GCSE in
Applied Science
for OCR

John Beeby
Jackie Clegg
David Lees
Chris Sherry

Series editor:
Bob McDuell

www.heinemann.co.uk
✓ Free online support
✓ Useful weblinks
✓ 24 hour online ordering

01865 888058

Heinemann Educational Publishers
Halley Court, Jordan Hill, Oxford OX2 8EJ
Part of Harcourt Education

Heinemann is a registered trademark of
Harcourt Education Limited

© John Beeby, Jackie Clegg, David Lees, Chris Sherry, 2003, 2006

First published 2003
Revised edition 2006

11 10 09 08 07 06
10 9 8 7 6 5 4 3 2 1

British Library Cataloguing in Publication Data is available from the
British Library on request.

10-digit ISBN 0 435 47091 4
13-digit ISBN 978 0 435 47091 3

Edited by Tim Jackson and Patrick Bonham

Designed by Gecko

Original illustrations © Harcourt Education Limited, 2003, 2006

Typeset and illustrated by Tech-Set Ltd, Gateshead, Tyne and Wear

Printed by Scotprint Ltd.

Cover photos: Corbis

Picture research by Maria Joannou

Acknowledgements

Every effort has been made to contact copyright holders of material reproduced in this book. Any omissions will be rectified in subsequent printings if notice is given to the publishers.

The authors and publishers would like to thank the following for permission to use photographs:

T = top, **B** = bottom, **L** = left, **R** = right, **M** = middle

SPL = Science Photo Library

Cover: Corbis

Student Book Acknowledgements

Page 2, **T** Beeby Education Limited ×2; 4, **B** SPL/Jeurgen Berger; 4 **T** Cephas; 5, Cephas; 6, **T** Pete Morris; 6, **B** Anthony Blake ×2; 7, Harourt/Peter Gould; 8, **L** SPL/St Mary's Hospital; 8, **R** SPL/Maxmillan Stock; 9, Wellcome Trust; 10, **T** Holt Studios; 10, **M** Garden Matters; 10, **B** Pete Morris; 11, Ancient Art & Architecture; 12, **T** SPL/Litchfield; 12, **M** SPL/Moulds; 14, SPL; 16, Holt Studios ×2; 19, Rothampstead Research; Institute; 24, Secretts Nursery; 25, **TL** Garden Picture Library; 25 **TR** Holt Studios; 26, Holt Studios ×2; 28, **M** Holt Studios; 28, **T** SPL/Sauze; 28, **B** SPL/Jeremy Burgess; 29, SPL/Michler; 30, **T** Holt Studios; 30, **M** SPL/Barksdale; 32, SPL/Nuridsany/Perennou; 33, Agripicture/Peter Dean; 35, **T** Corbis/Naturfoto Honal/Klaus Honal; 35, **B** Corbis/ John Wilkinson/Ecoscene; 36, **T** Greenpeace/ Archivo Museo Salesiano; 36 **B** Greenpeace/Daniel Beltra/De Agostini; 37, Alamy/ David Boag; 38, **T** Holt Studios; 38, **B** SPL/Menzel; 39, SPL/Agstock; 40, **TR** Holt Studios; 40, **TL** Alamy; 40, **BL** Science Photo Library; 40, **BR** SPL; 42, Pete Morris; 44, Holt Studios; 45, SPL/CNRI; 46 Holt Studios; 48, SPL/Tompinkson; 50, SPL/Rosenfield Images; 51, Photofusion; 52, **T** Garden Picture Library; 52, **B** Pete Morris; 54, Beeby Education Limited ×2; 58, **T** Rex Features/Shout; 58 **B** Alamy/Shout; 59, SPL/ Michael Donne; 60, SPL/CC Studio; 62, SPL/James King-Holmes; 68, SPL/Plailly; 70, SPL/Doug Martin; 71, SPL/National Cancer Institute; 72, Action Plus; 73, Empics; 74, SPL/Terry&Sheasby; 75, SPL/Eye of Science; 76, SPL/BSIP VEM; 77, SPL/Saturn; 78, **T** Mediscan; 78, **B** SPL/Peter Arnold Ind; 79, SPL/Nuridsany&Perennou; 80, **T** Photofusion; 80, **B** SPL/CCStudio; 82, **T** Harcourt/Gareth Boden; 82, **M** SPL; 83, Roger Scruton/Harcourt; 84, S&R Greenhill ×2; 86, **M** SPL/James Stevenson; 86, **B** Guzelian; 89, Rex Features/Sipa Press; 90, **T** SPL/Mauro Fermariello; 90, **M** SPL/James King Holmes; 94, Pete Morris; 96, **T** Capital Pictures; 96, **B** Still Pictures; 97, Robert Harding; 98, Peter Gould ×2; 100, **T** SPL/Bond; 100, **M** Corbis; 101, Peter Gould; 104, **TL** Corbis; 104, **TR** SPL/Adam Hart-Davis; 104, **M** Peter Gould; 105, Peter Gould ×3; 106, SPL; 108, **T** Alamy; 108, **BL** Roger Scruton/Harcourt; 108, **BR** Harcourt; 109, **T** Harcourt; 109, **B** SPL/Fraser; 110, Peter Gould; 111, Anthony Blake; 112, Photofusion; 114, SPL/Agstock; 117, **T** Corbis/Annie Griffiths Belt; 117, **M** Alamy/ Henry Westheim Photography; 118, **T** SPL/Guyon; 118, **M** SPL/ Biophoto Associates; 119, Alamy/G P Bowater; 120, Alamy; 120, **M/B** Peter Gould ×2; 124, Alamy; 125, JURIJ SKRLJ Photography; 126, Pete Morris ×3; 127, Car Photo Library; 128, **T** SPL; 128, **M** SPL; 128, **B** Corbis; 129, **T** Alamy/Geogphotos; 129, SPL; 130, **T** John Wamsley; 130, **M** Pete Morris; 131, **T** Pete Morris; 131, **ML** Corbis, 131, **MR** Shout; 132, **T** Corbis; 132, **M** Christie's Images; 134, Empics ×2; 136, **T** Apple Mac; 136, **M** Nokia; 136, **B** SPL/Knapton; 137, Motoring Picture Library; 138, **T** Photodisc; 138, **M** Pete Morris; 138, **B** SPL/Biophoto; 142, Construction Photography/ DIY Photolibrary; 146, Author Supplied ×2; 148, **T** AP; 148 **ML** Milepost 92½; 148, **MR** SPL/Knapton; 150, **T** SPL/Chassenet; 150, **B** SPL/Fraser; 152, Photofusion; 153, Nirex/BNFL ×2; 154, **T** Photo Library of Wales; 154, **B** Robert Harding; 155, Photo Library of Wales; 156, **T** SPL/NASA; 156, **M** SPL/Bartel; 158, Peter Thompson Photography ×2; 160, **T** Corbis; 160, **M** Photodisc; 160, **B** Corbis/Roy Morsch; 161, Motoring Picture Library; 163, SPL/bond; 164, Calor Gas; 165, PA Photos; 166, Elizabeth Whiting; 168, Redferns/Hayley Madden; 169, Redferns/ Hayley Madden ×2; 170, Pete Morris; 171, **M** Robert Harding; 171, Interior Archive ×2; 172, SPL/Pasieka; 174, Robert Harding; 176, Photodisc; 177, Car Photo Library; 178, Pete Morris ×2; 179, Pete Morris; 182, **T** Mentorn TV; 182, **M** SPL/Maxmillan Stock; 182, **B** Corbis; 183, Shout; 184, SPL/Ashfield; 186, SPL/Parker; 189, **M** Alamy/PHOTOTAKE Inc; 189, **B** Alamy/Peter Arnold, Inc; 190, **ML** Alamy/ Profimedia; 190, **M** Sony Ericsson; 190, **MR** Alamy/ David Gould; 191, SPL/ Dr Arthur Tucker; 192, Author Supplied; 196, Topham Picturepoint; 198,Corbis/Jon Sparks; 199, **M** Ecoscene/Jon Bower; 199, **B** SPL/David Hay Jones; 200, Alamy; 201, Getty Images/Robert Harding; 202, SPL ×2; 203, SPL; 204, **T** NASA/COBE/ NSSDC; 204, **M** SPL; 205, NASA; 206, Rex Features/Novosti.

Student CD-ROM

© Heinemann Educational Publishers 2003, 2006.
The material in this publication is copyright. It may be edited and printed for one-time use as instructional material in a classroom by a teacher, but may not be copied in unlimited quantities, kept on behalf of others, passed on or sold to third parties, or stored for future use in a retrieval system. If you wish to use the material in any way other than that specified you must apply in writing to the publisher.

Student CD ROM Acknowledgements

Section 1.5, SPL; 1.17, (Global Temperature Graph). Copyright of the Climatic Research Unit, School of Environmental Sciences at the University of East Anglia - http://www.cru.uea.ac.uk/cru/info/warming; 1.17, (Question containing bird egg laying graph) Nest Record Scheme of the British Trust for Ornithology; 1.19, Bernard Kettlewell; 1.22, Pete Morris; 3.13 (1), **T** Rex Features; 3.13, **M** Getty Images/ Stone; 3.13 (2), Still Pictures/ Mark Edwards; 3.13 (3), Still Pictures/ Mark Edwards; 4.5 (1), **TL** Photodisc; 4.5 (1), **TR** Chris Honeywell; 5.15 (2), **T** Trevor Clifford; 5.15 (2), **B** Corbis; 5.22 (1), Alamy Images/worldthroughthelens; 6.4 (1), SPL; 6.4 (2), SPL; Science in the workplace (1), SPL; Science in the workplace (3), **T** SPL; Science in the workplace (3), **M** SPL; Science in the workplace – making painkillers (1), SPL ×2.

Acrobat ® Reader™Copyright © 1987–2003 Adobe Systems Incorporated and its licensors. All rights reserved. Adobe, the Adobe logo, Acrobat, the Acrobat logo, PostScript, and the PostScript logo are either registered trademarks or trademarks of Adobe Systems Incorporated in the United States and/or other countries.

Navigation, menu and help pages created by TAG Publishing Services

Technical Problems

If you encounter technical problems whilst running this software, please contact the Customer Support team by ringing 01865 888108 or e-mailing secondary.enquiries@harcourteducation.co.uk.

Units and portfolio tasks

OCR Applied Science for GCSE looks at the science and scientific skills we use in everyday life. Many people who would not call themselves scientists use a great deal of science every day.

Your GCSE Applied Science course is made up of three units. Each unit carries the same number of marks and so is equally important.

What the units are

Unit 1 is called 'Developing scientific skills'. For this unit you produce a portfolio of work as part of your coursework. You will carry out the sort of practical procedures scientists and technicians perform in their jobs. There are three areas:

- Investigating living organisms
- Chemical analysis
- Investigating materials.

Unit 2 is called 'Science for the needs of society'. This unit includes the important ideas and issues in science today. Unit 2 covers the national curriculum for core science including biology, chemistry and physics. You will sit an exam for this part of the course.

Unit 3 is called 'Science at work'. You will produce a portfolio of your work for this unit as well. This unit looks at people using science in their jobs and in industry.

As you can see, Unit 2 is the only part of the qualification for which you have to sit an exam. You can study Unit 2 at either Foundation Level or Higher Level, but your level of entry does not limit the final grade that you can achieve. Two-thirds of your total marks for Applied Science come from your portfolios. This means that even if you do the Foundation exam in Unit 2, if you produce good portfolios you could get a grade higher than C. So producing good portfolios is very important. But don't worry: we give you lots of help to do all of this.

Portfolio tasks

You need to produce coursework for both Units 1 and 3. The coursework is divided into **portfolio tasks**, which can be investigations, practical tasks or research. When you have completed a task, you can add it to your portfolio. You should look at your portfolio and make sure it contains only your best work. Only your best work will be evaluated.

With portfolios, the quality of what you do is often more important than the quantity. Make sure you have a copy of the criteria your teacher will use to mark your work.

This book and Student CD-ROM will help you achieve the best you can in this qualification. The next two pages show you how.

How this course supports OCR Applied Science

The qualification is made up of three units. This course provides you with support for each unit:

Unit 2   This textbook covers all of Unit 2 at Foundation tier. The Higher tier material can be found on the Student CD-ROM that comes with this book.

Units 1 and 3   These units are assessed on the portfolio that you will produce. The Teacher CD-ROM gives lots of help with portfolio tasks (see below).

This textbook also includes essential knowledge and skills for Units 1 and 3.

How to use this book and Student CD-ROM

There are six chapters in the book. Each chapter follows the same format:

Introductory Case Study

Each chapter starts with a case study showing how the science you are going to read about in the book is used by real people in their working lives. The introduction also clearly lists the linked portfolio work for Units 1 and 3, which is available on the Teacher CD-ROM.

Main pages

These introduce ideas in science and how they are used in the real world. Quick questions throughout the double-page spreads help you to check that you have understood what you have read. At the end of each section there are one or more tasks. These are questions based on what you have just learned.

Higher tier material

Sometimes you will also find a symbol like this one:

The **H** tells you that there is Higher tier material on this topic, the ⊙ CD-ROM tells you that you can find it on the CD-ROM that comes with this book. Unless you are doing Higher Level you do not need to look at the extra **H** material on the Student CD-ROM.

A page of higher tier text on the Student CD-ROM looks similar to a page in the Student book.

    a What has happened to the date at which robins have started laying eggs?

    b Suggest how this might be linked to changes in mean temperatures since 1940.

    c Give one more example of an organism that has been affected by changes in seasonal temperatures.

1.18 Getting the best out of animals

1 Some farmers use intensive farming methods to raise pigs. Explain why these pigs grow more quickly than pigs raised by more natural methods.

1.19 Selective breeding

1 A farmer is selectively breeding his cows to increase the milk yield from his herd.

    a Write down the meaning of the term 'selective breeding'.

    b Describe the different stages of the selective breeding programme carried out by the farmer.

    c Suggest one other feature a farmer may wish to selectively breed into his animals.

1.20 Cross-breeding

1 Explain the difference between cross-breeding and selective breeding.

1.22 Genetics 2

1 Explain the difference between chromosomes and genes.

2 Tim keeps pet rabbits. When Tim mated two black rabbits, some of the babies were black and some were white. In the questions, use **B** as the dominant allele for black fur, and **b** as the recessive allele for white fur.

    a Tim concluded that the parents must both carry a recessive allele. Give reasons for Tim's decision.

    b Copy and complete the Punnett square to show the possible genotype of the offspring.

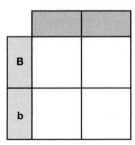

    c For Tim's baby rabbits, write down the ratio of black fur babies to white fur babies.

At the very end of the Tasks box you may find this symbol:

More questions (CD-ROM)

This symbol tells you that you can find Higher tier questions on your CD-ROM. These questions are based on the material in the section you are looking at, but are more challenging than the questions in the Tasks box. You only need to attempt these if you are taking the Higher tier paper for Unit 2.

1.23 Genetic engineering

1 James is diabetic. He needs to inject insulin into his body twice a day. For many years this insulin has been extracted from the pancreas of cattle, sheep and pigs. Scientists are now able to produce human insulin using genetic engineering.

The diagram shows some of the stages involved in the production of genetically engineered human insulin.

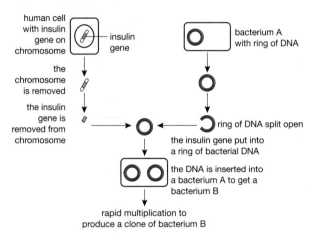

a Describe how the insulin gene is removed from the human chromosome.
b The clone of bacterium 2 produces large quantities of insulin.
  i Describe what is meant by the term 'clone'.
  ii Explain why bacteria are suitable organisms to use for this purpose.
c Explain the advantages of genetically engineered insulin compared with insulin extracted from animals.

1.24 GM crops

1 Here is a newspaper cutting about GM crops.

> **Biotech Crops May Aid Farmers**
> A study on the impact of GM crops indicated that Kansas and Missouri farmers could significantly improve their income with such crops.

a Describe what is meant by the term 'GM crops'.
b Suggest why GM crops could improve the income of farmers.
c Suggest why some people do not like the idea of introducing GM crops into our farmland.

Information for units 1 and 3

Sometimes there is more in a section than you need for Unit 2. The extra material is there to help you with your portfolio work, but you do not need to learn it for your Unit 2 exam. It is indicated by a light yellow tint.

3.9 Chrome yellow

No parking!

When you walk through any city centre you see yellow lines on most of the roads. The lines show where motorists are not allowed to park their cars.

a Suggest why this yellow is used for the lines which show where cars cannot be parked.

The yellow colour for these lines is due to a **pigment** called lead chromate or chrome yellow. It is the same pigment that van Gogh used in his sunflower paintings.

Making lead chromate

Solutions of lead nitrate and sodium chromate mixed together make lead chromate. A deep yellow solid is formed. A solid that is formed when two solutions are mixed together is called a **precipitate**. The correct description for our solid is a yellow precipitate.

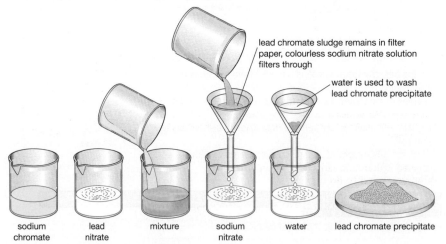

lead chromate sludge remains in filter paper, colourless sodium nitrate solution filters through

water is used to wash lead chromate precipitate

sodium chromate   lead nitrate   mixture   sodium nitrate   water   lead chromate precipitate

sodium chromate + lead nitrate → lead chromate + sodium nitrate

Great care has to be taken when lead chromate is made. It is very poisonous and may cause a range of effects, including kidney damage, impaired eyesight, nerve damage and cancer.

b Suggest what simple safety precautions are taken when lead chromate is made.

112

Portfolio work

Sometimes your work on the tasks at the end of a double-page spread can contribute to your portfolio. In such cases, the reference to the particular objective that the task fulfils is given beneath, for example: *Portfolio Unit 3*.

Often there will be **portfolio tasks** on the Teacher CD-ROM related to the material on the spread. These are listed in the Tasks box, along with the objectives they fulfil. This symbol tells you that your teacher can look up the task on their CD-ROM.

Activity 24 ————————— H C E

Heater

Application

You may have a radiant heater in your house or in your school. Radiant heaters have *heating elements*. They glow red-hot when a current passes through them.

The heating element is a coil of nichrome resistance wire wound onto an insulated bar. Each element in this radiant heater has a power rating of 1000 W.

The resistance of the wire used to make each element is about 60 Ω.

Aim of the activity

The resistance of a wire depends on:
- the material the wire is made from;
- the length of the wire;
- the cross-sectional area (or diameter) of the wire.

You are going to investigate how these factors affect the resistance of a wire.

Risk assessment

Read through the instructions for this activity. Carry out a risk assessment using a Risk Assessment sheet. Ask your teacher to check this before you begin.

> #### Safety
> Be careful – the nichrome wire may get very hot and may start a fire. If you burn yourself on the wire, get cold running water onto the burn as quickly as possible.

Equipment
Ammeter
Voltmeter
Nichrome wire of diameter 0.160 mm, 0.200 mm, 0.250 mm, 0.315 mm and 0.400 mm (or 28 SWG, 30 SWG, 32 SWG, 34 SWG, 36 SWG and 38 SWG)
Constantan or manganin wire of similar diameters

What you need to do

1 Set up the circuit shown in **Background info 24**. Investigate the resistance of different materials (nichrome and constantan or manganin). Look at the **Aim** of the activity. What **two** variables need to be kept the same?

2 Record your results in a table like the first one on **Results sheet 24H**.

3 Use the same apparatus to investigate the resistance of different lengths of 0.160 mm (or 38 SWG) nichrome wire, from 20 cm to 100 cm, at 20 cm intervals. What **two** variables are you keeping the same?

4 Record your results in a table like the second one on **Results sheet 24H**.

5 Plot a graph of resistance against length. You can use the graph paper on **Results sheet 24H**.

End-of-chapter case study

Each chapter also ends with a case study to give you lots of ideas about how people use the science you have learned.

End-of-chapter questions

At the end of each chapter there are three pages of exam-style questions for Foundation tier students. The questions on the first page are written for grades G–E. The questions on the second page are for grades D–C.

On the Student CD-ROM you will find Higher tier exam-style questions. These are based on all the content – in the Student book and on the Student CD-ROM. You should do these questions if you are entered for the Higher Level examination.

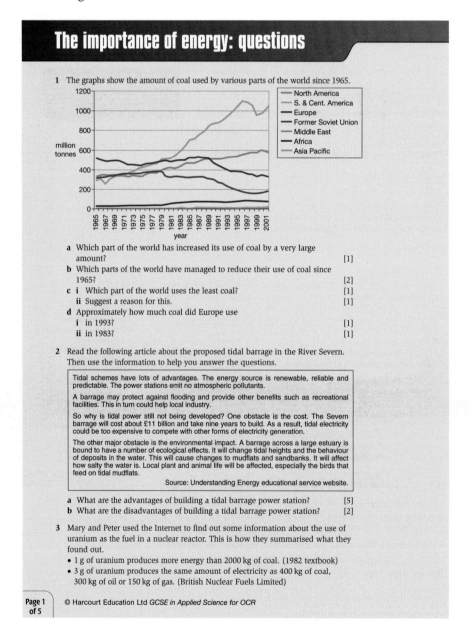

The importance of energy: questions

1 The graphs show the amount of coal used by various parts of the world since 1965.

Legend:
- North America
- S. & Cent. America
- Europe
- Former Soviet Union
- Middle East
- Africa
- Asia Pacific

y-axis: million tonnes (0 to 1200)
x-axis: year (1965 to 2001)

a Which part of the world has increased its use of coal by a very large amount? [1]

b Which parts of the world have managed to reduce their use of coal since 1965? [2]

c i Which part of the world uses the least coal? [1]
   ii Suggest a reason for this. [1]

d Approximately how much coal did Europe use
   i in 1993? [1]
   ii in 1983? [1]

2 Read the following article about the proposed tidal barrage in the River Severn. Then use the information to help you answer the questions.

> Tidal schemes have lots of advantages. The energy source is renewable, reliable and predictable. The power stations emit no atmospheric pollutants.
>
> A barrage may protect against flooding and provide other benefits such as recreational facilities. This in turn could help local industry.
>
> So why is tidal power still not being developed? One obstacle is the cost. The Severn barrage will cost about £11 billion and take nine years to build. As a result, tidal electricity could be too expensive to compete with other forms of electricity generation.
>
> The other major obstacle is the environmental impact. A barrage across a large estuary is bound to have a number of ecological effects. It will change tidal heights and the behaviour of deposits in the water. This will cause changes to mudflats and sandbanks. It will affect how salty the water is. Local plant and animal life will be affected, especially the birds that feed on tidal mudflats.
>
> Source: Understanding Energy educational service website.

a What are the advantages of building a tidal barrage power station? [5]
b What are the disadvantages of building a tidal barrage power station? [2]

3 Mary and Peter used the Internet to find out some information about the use of uranium as the fuel in a nuclear reactor. This is how they summarised what they found out.
   • 1 g of uranium produces more energy than 2000 kg of coal. (1982 textbook)
   • 3 g of uranium produces the same amount of electricity as 400 kg of coal, 300 kg of oil or 150 kg of gas. (British Nuclear Fuels Limited)

Student CD-ROM

This is a brief outline of just some of the things you will find on the Student CD-ROM:

- **How to compile your portfolio**

  This gives you guidance on how to build a portfolio.

- **Research bank**

  This resource includes case studies on local, national and international industries. With information and questions to get you started on your research, the research bank will help you with your portfolio work for Unit 3.

- **Interactive self-assessment tests**

  These are informal tests based on Unit 2. They are done onscreen and give you instant feedback on your progress.

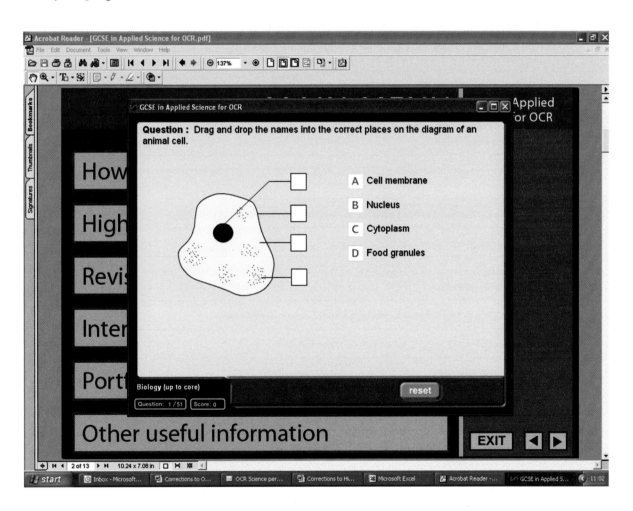

- **Higher tier**

  This includes all you need to know to achieve a grade B–A* in your Unit 2 exam.

- **Revision checklists**

  Checklists that tell you what you need to be able to do for Unit 2. You can tick off things you have learned as you go through the course.

Revision checklists – Biology

	1. Using living organisms		
	Tick column **A** when you have covered the statement in class. Tick column **B** when you are confident you can answer any questions on it. In your revision for Unit 2, test on those statements not ticked. Statements in **bold** can only appear on the Higher Tier paper. I can	A	B
1	identify useful products that can be made from living things.		
2	recall that wool, silk, cotton, leather, medicines and dyes are all obtained from living organisms.		
3	identify the uses of fermentation and use a word equation to describe fermentation in yeast.		
4	**state the balanced symbol equation for fermentation in yeast.**		
5	describe an enzyme as a biological catalyst.		
6	describe how enzymes are involved in the brewing, baking and dairy industries, and in penicillin production.		
7	**explain why fermentation works better under certain conditions.**		
8	describe the cell as the common feature of all organisms.		
9	describe living organisms as being made up of chemical compounds.		
10	**recall that all living organisms are made up of carbohydrates, proteins, lipids and nucleic acid.**		
11	**explain why viruses do not conform to this model.**		
12	identify the parts of the cell and their functions.		
13	state the location and structure of chromosomes and that they carry the cell's genetic information.		
14	state that genes are made up of DNA which carries the genetic code.		
15	describe the similarities and differences between plant and animal cells.		

Teacher CD-ROM

On the Teacher CD-ROM there are a range of suitable Portfolio tasks for Units 1 and 3. Tasks are written at up to three different levels (lower, intermediate and higher) so that you can work at the right level for you and get the most out of the course.

Some of the tasks are for Unit 1. These are practical and may involve work in the laboratory.

Tasks for Unit 3 are about science in the workplace. You may need to do research for these. The research bank on the Student CD-ROM will help you with this.

Contents

Chapter 6: The Earth and Universe

Units and symbols you need to know

Equations and formulae

Glossary

Index

Using living organisms

Case study: Brewing beer at Brewster's Brewery

We use microorganisms to make many food products. One of these food products is beer. Sara Barton runs Brewster's Brewery near Melton Mowbray.

Sara at Brewster's Brewery.

Getting qualified

Sara is a trained biochemist. After A levels, she did a biochemistry degree, and then a master's degree in brewing at Heriot-Watt University. 'Many small brewers start with an interest in home brewing', explains Sara, 'but I went to university to get qualified'. After university, she worked for three years with a national brewer. Sara then joined a **pharmaceutical company**. 'But my first love was brewing', says Sara, 'and in 1998 I decided to set up my own brewery.' While she was working, Sara did a business degree in her spare time. She then felt confident to deal with the business side of running a brewery.

The ingredients

Sara brews around 50 barrels of beer a week. The ingredients used to brew beer are yeast, malted barley, hops and water. To brew her beers, she has specially selected a type of brewers' yeast that gives Brewster's beers a fruity taste and smell. This type of yeast grows well during the brewing process. It's also easy to separate out after the beer has been brewed.

Malted barley, or malt, provides the yeast with the sugar it needs to grow. The yeast turns the sugar into alcohol and carbon dioxide. Sara uses malt made from a variety of barley called Maris Otter. Sara chose Maris Otter because of the flavour it gives to beer.

The brewhouse at Brewster's Brewery.

Hops make the beer bitter, but they also provide its aroma. Sara uses several different varieties of hops. To produce a bitter beer, she uses old English varieties that have been around for over a hundred years. For her summer beers, which have a citrus taste, she selects the latest varieties of hops bred in England and America.

One of the most important ingredients of beer is water. Sara adjusts the chemical composition of the brewing water so that it's just right for brewing her beer.

Sara makes sure that the brewing process itself – fermentation – is carefully controlled. She brews her beers at 20–21 °C for four to five days.

When the process is complete, the beer is run into barrels or bottles. Brewster's Brewery sells its beer locally – in Leicestershire, Cambridgeshire and Lincolnshire, but Sara is expanding her trade into other counties.

1 What qualifications does Sara have to help her understand the science of the brewing process?

2 What additional skills help her to run Brewster's Brewery?

3 What qualities does Sara look for in:
   a the yeast she uses
   b the variety of malt she uses
   c the variety of hops she uses?

4 At what temperature does she brew her beer?

How this chapter can help you with your portfolio

Unit I CD-ROM

You will learn about the uses of living organisms, their cells and life processes in this chapter, which will help you with these portfolio tasks:

● Using aseptic technique to culture yeast cells
● Making yogurt
● Investigating the effect of different antibiotics on the growth of bacteria
● Setting up a light microscope to examine plant cells
● Setting up a light microscope to examine fibres
● Setting up a light microscope to examine yeast cells
● Cloning a plant

Unit 3 CD-ROM

This chapter will also help you with these portfolio tasks:

● Monitoring the growth of a microorganism, plant or animal

This chapter will help you to understand these case studies on your CD-ROM:

● Brewing
● Silk farm
● Making painkillers
● Hydroponics

1.1 Brewing beer

People have been making bread and beer for 8000 years. Today, bakers and brewers use science to help them to improve the production process.

Fermentation

Bread and beer are made using the same chemical reaction. It is called **fermentation**.

Fermentation converts the sugar glucose into alcohol and carbon dioxide.

glucose (sugar) → ethanol (alcohol) + carbon dioxide

Fermentation is a special kind of respiration where no oxygen is present. A microscopic fungus called yeast is added when you are making both bread and beer.

a What organism is used to produce beer?

Chemical reactions in organisms such as yeast produce useful products like beer. But these chemical reactions would be too slow without the help of **enzymes**. Enzymes are biological catalysts.

Catalysts are chemicals that speed up chemical reactions. Although catalysts take part in reactions, they are unchanged at the end of the reactions and can be used over and over again.

Checking the temperature of the brew.

To make beer, the brewer mixes malted barley grains with warm water. Hops are added. After heating, the liquid is then cooled. It is run into the fermenter and the yeast is added. After a while, the air in the fermenter runs out. This is necessary for fermentation.

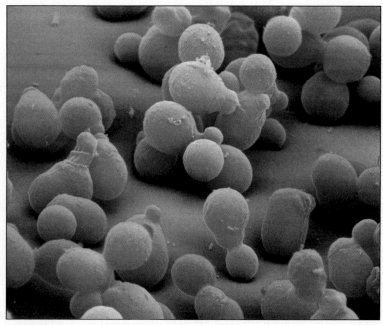

Yeast cells.

Controlling reactions

The yeast has all the conditions it needs to grow, including a supply of sugar and a suitable temperature. The temperature is kept between 15°C and 25°C. These are the temperatures at which the yeast's enzymes work best.

- If the fermentation temperature is too low, the enzymes will be inactive.
- If the temperature is too high, the enzymes will be destroyed.

b Why is the liquid cooled before the yeast is added?

The fermentation stops when the sugar runs out. The brewer then puts the beer into barrels or bottles.

Fermentation of the wort (the mixture of malt, hops and water).

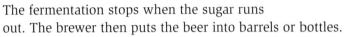 **More on brewing and enzymes**

TASKS

1 a List the conditions that yeast needs for fermentation.
  b What are the chemicals found in yeast that speed up the fermentation process?
  c When barley is malted, the starch in the grains is broken down into sugar. What chemicals help to speed up the malting process?

2 Any fruit or vegetable that contains sugar can be fermented using yeast to produce an alcoholic drink.
  a Find out which alcoholic drinks are made by fermentation.
  b Find out what these drinks are made from.

3 **Setting up a light microscope to examine yeast cells**
  Portfolio Unit 1

4 **Using aseptic technique to culture yeast cells**
  Portfolio Unit 1

5 **Brewing beer**
  Portfolio Unit 1

6 **Monitoring the activity of yeast during the brewing process**
  Portfolio Unit 1, Unit 3

7 **Brewing**
  Portfolio Unit 3

 **More questions**

1.2 Making bread and yogurt

Bread and yogurt are made in very different ways. But both need enzymes.

Bread

Around the world, bread is mostly made from the cereals wheat, rye, maize, millet, oats or barley.

Different sorts of bread.

Bread is made using the same process of fermentation as is used in brewing beer.

John, a baker, first mixes his flour with yeast, water and sugar to make dough.

a What food substance does the yeast need?

The baker leaves the dough in a warm place. Enzymes in the yeast change the sugar into alcohol and carbon dioxide. The dough gets bigger. It is the trapped carbon dioxide gas that causes the dough to rise.

Before . . .

. . . and after.

b Why does the baker allow the bread to stand?

c Why is this done in a warm place and not in the refrigerator?

When the bread is baked in a hot oven, the ethanol (alcohol) evaporates. The bubbles of gas expand, giving the bread a light texture.

d When the yeast ferments in the bread, it makes ethanol. What happens to this ethanol when the bread is cooked?

Yogurt

Yogurt is a kind of curdled milk.

Brewing and baking use enzymes from yeast. Yogurt is made using different enzymes. They come from bacteria that are added to the milk. Chemicals produced by the bacteria give the yogurt its slightly sour taste.

To make yogurt, it is important that the milk is kept at 45°C in order for the bacteria to grow.

The enzymes involved in making yogurt like higher temperatures than those preferred by enzymes in yeast. Unlike the catalysts used in the chemicals industry, very few biological catalysts work at temperatures above 55°C.

 **More on enzymes**

TASKS

1 Where does the sugar for fermentation come from in the production of:
   a bread   b beer   c yogurt?

2 In some types of bread, no yeast is added. How would this type of bread differ from normal bread?

3 Look at these statements.
   • are destroyed by heat
   • are unchanged during the reaction
   • are used in the chemical industry
   • can work at very high temperatures.
   From the statements above, write down the statements that are true about:
   a catalysts   b enzymes.

4 **Making yogurt**
   Portfolio Unit 1

Bacteria, like yeast, are microorganisms.

Antibiotics like penicillin are drugs that help your body to fight bacteria. They kill the bacteria causing infection in the body. They do not work on infections caused by viruses.

a What is an antibiotic?

b What kind of microorganism do antibiotics kill?

The first modern antibiotic

Antibiotics are obtained from microorganisms like moulds. In 1928, Alexander Fleming, in a London hospital, discovered a mould that was able to kill bacteria in a **Petri dish**. He identified the mould as a kind of *Penicillium*. He called the chemical that he made from the mould **penicillin**.

Alexander Fleming in his laboratory.

Penicillin production.

Fleming found that penicillin could kill bacteria that caused many infections in patients.

Penicillin was first used to treat infection in the 1940s. In those days, you had to have a large injection of it instead of taking tablets or capsules! But it was a miracle drug. Suddenly, incurable diseases could be cured. Often it took only one dose. Penicillin saved the lives of thousands of soldiers in the Second World War, and millions more people since.

c How would you have taken a dose of penicillin in the 1940s?

d How would you take penicillin today?

e What effect did penicillin have on the treatment of disease?

Antibiotics today

To produce penicillin today, *Penicillium* mould is grown in tall reactors. The mould is fed glucose and ammonia. The reactor is kept at 25°C.

f What can you suggest about the way the enzymes in *Penicillium* work?

The penicillin family of antibiotics is still the most important today. Many new forms of the drug have been made that kill a wide range of bacteria.

Today, scientists continue to look for new, improved antibiotics. Many scientists investigate natural chemicals found in living organisms, just as scientists have done for a hundred years. If a new antibiotic kills bacteria in a Petri dish, it must then be tested to see if it's toxic. If it isn't toxic, it's then tested to see if it will kill bacteria in laboratory animals, and then in human infections. Pharmaceutical companies must trial new antibiotics for several years to make sure that they are completely safe and do not produce side effects.

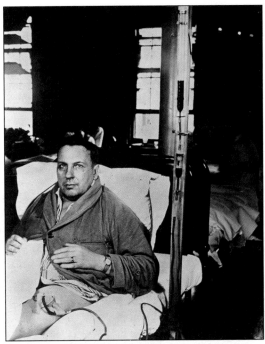

A patient being given impure penicillin of early manufacture (note its dark colour) by intramuscular infusion. Nowadays we just take tablets or capsules!

More on treating disease CD-ROM

TASKS

1 a What are chemicals called that kill bacteria?
   b When were these chemicals first discovered?

2 Alexander Fleming discovered the chemical penicillin but could not make it in the large quantities needed to treat people.
   Try to find out who first succeeded in doing this.

3 Why shouldn't doctors prescribe antibiotics for a cold?

4 Explain what would happen to penicillin production if *Penicillium* mould was kept at:
   a 0°C   b 55°C

5 Explain why, when penicillin was first isolated and tested, in the late 1930s and early 1940s:
   a Researcher J.M. Barnes injected two mice with broth containing penicillin.
   b Fifty mice were injected with *Staphylococcus* bacteria. Twenty-five of the mice were then injected with the broth containing penicillin.
   c Penicillin was first tested on a human who had blood poisoning and was close to death.

6 **Using microorganisms safely in the laboratory**
   Portfolio Unit 1, Unit 3 CD-ROM

7 **Investigating the effect of different antibiotics on the growth of bacteria**
   Portfolio Unit 1, Unit 3 CD-ROM

More questions CD-ROM

We get many useful products from plants and animals.

Plants

Plants are used to make and colour clothing.

Cotton is picked from the cotton plant. It is spun into yarn and made into cloth.

The blue dye for jeans can come either from the woad plant or from a dye made from coal tar.

a What can be made from the woad plant?

Many dyes and pigments come from plants. Some hair dyes and dyes for tattoos come from the leaves of the henna plant.

b What is made from the henna plant?

Scientists study plants to try to get new medicines and drugs to fight diseases. Morphine or opium poppies are used to make the painkiller, morphine.

The Earth's rainforests contain about half of the known plant species. They are likely to be a rich source of medicinal drugs. Large areas of rainforest are being cleared to make way for farmland and new homes. As this happens, many species of plants that scientists have not yet studied may become extinct.

c How could the destruction of the rainforests affect the search for new medicines?

The cotton cloth is dyed. The cloth is used to make jeans.

Animals

We use the fleeces of sheep to make wool. Wool is used to make warm clothes. The skin of cows is also used for clothing, such as shoes. It is called leather.

Silk worms produce silk. Silk can be coloured and woven to make clothes and tapestries.

A silk tapestry.

d Wool, leather and silk are made using animals. For which of these does the animal need to be killed?

e For each of wool, leather and silk, write down one item of clothing that can be made using it.

TASKS

1 Name three drinks that are made from plants.

2 From the plant products below, make two lists:

List 1: Natural products
List 2: Processed products

baked beans	banana	Brussels sprouts	charcoal
coffee beans	cork	olive oil	onions
paper	pepper	rubber	sweet corn
tea leaves	tobacco		

3 Name three products made from animals.

4 **Making painkillers**
   Portfolio Unit 3 CD-ROM

5 **Silk farm**
   Portfolio Unit 3 CD-ROM

 **More questions**
CD-ROM

1.5 Cells

Where do we find cells?

The cotton in your clothes is made from a plant. If you look at it under a powerful microscope, this is what it looks like.

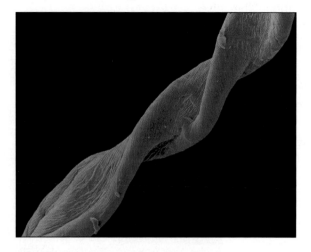

Nylon is made from crude oil. It is called a **synthetic** fibre. The picture on the right shows what it looks like under a powerful microscope.

a What differences can you see between the structures of cotton and nylon?

Cotton, like all plants, is made up of cells. Nylon is not made from a plant and is not made up of cells.

All plants and animals are made up of cells. These cells vary in size, but only the largest cells are visible to our naked eye. A microscope is needed to see detail in *any* cell.

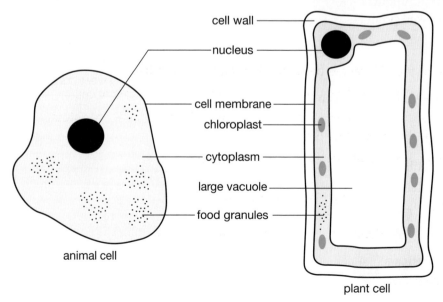

animal cell

plant cell

Components of cells

Nucleus is the control centre of the cell. It contains tiny thread-like structures called **chromosomes**. The chromosomes are strings of **genes**. Genes carry genetic information. They give instructions to our cells. The instructions make us function and control how we look.

Cell membrane – controls what substances enter and leave the cell. Cells need to bring in chemicals like water to stay alive. Cells produce waste substances, which need to be taken out of the cell.

Cell wall – keeps the cell a rigid shape.

Cytoplasm – is where the chemical reactions that keep the cell alive take place here.

Chloroplasts – contain the green pigment **chlorophyll**. Chlorophyll absorbs light energy, which the plant needs to make its food.

Vacuoles – in plant cells may be large, permanent structures filled with cell sap, which is water and dissolved chemicals. The vacuole helps keep the plant cells firm.

b What are the large vacuoles in plant cells for?

c What do the cell membranes in both plants and animals do?

When an organism grows, its cells divide to produce more cells. All the new cells must be identical. To ensure this, the cells divide by a type of cell division called *mitosis*. Mitosis is also involved when cells or organisms are cloned. When an organism produces sex cells, or gametes, a different kind of cell division, called *meiosis*, is required.

Cell division

TASKS

1 Make a list of the differences between plant and animal cells.

2 Make a list of the parts of the cell that are in both plant and animal cells.

3 What are the structures in cells called that control things like the eye colour of an animal or the shape of leaves?

4 **Setting up a light microscope to examine plant cells**
   Portfolio Unit 1

5 **Setting up a light microscope to examine fibres**
   Portfolio Unit 1

6 **Setting up a light microscope to examine yeast cells**
   Portfolio Unit 1

More questions

All living things need food to live. Animals bring food into their bodies by eating and digesting it.

What is the panda eating?

Plants have a very different way of providing themselves with the energy to live and grow.
In an experiment, Jo grew a sunflower plant from seed.

Jo weighed a seed.

Jo weighed some compost.

Jo planted the seed.

Jo watered the seed.

After several months, Jo weighed the plant.

Jo weighed the soil from the pot.

The compost lost only 0.1 g in weight, but the plant's weight increased by 100 g! This means the plant did not get its food from the soil.

The sunflower had increased in weight because it was able to *make* its *own* food.

Photosynthesis

All plants make their own food by a process called **photosynthesis**. To carry out photosynthesis plants need:

- carbon dioxide from the air
- water from the soil
- light from the Sun
- chlorophyll: the green chemical that gives leaves their colour.

a Plants make their own food. What is this process called?

Photosynthesis mainly occurs in the leaves of plants.
Photosynthesis makes glucose, which is a kind of sugar. Glucose
is soluble. That means it dissolves in water. This means it can be
transported around the plant in solution.

When the plant wants to store food, it converts the glucose into
starch. Starch is insoluble. That means it doesn't dissolve in water
and can be stored.

b Why can't starch be transported around the plant?

The energy for photosynthesis comes from the Sun.
This diagram shows what happens during photosynthesis:

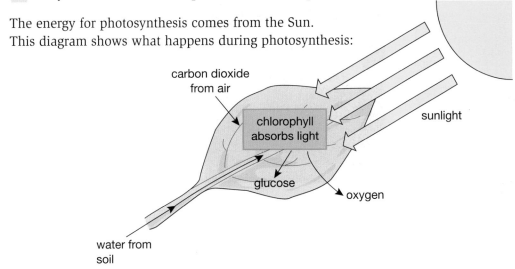

We can show photosynthesis as a word equation:

$$\text{carbon dioxide} + \text{water} \xrightarrow{\text{light and chlorophyll}} \text{glucose} + \text{oxygen}$$

c Where does the energy for photosynthesis come from?

TASKS

1 What four things do plants need to make their own food?

2 What is the name of the food that plants make? How is this food stored in plants?

3 During photosynthesis:
   a what gas is absorbed from the air?
   b what chemical is absorbed from the soil?
   c what waste gas is given out by the leaf?

Just like animals, plants need energy.

Why do plants need energy?

A plant needs energy to transport important chemicals, such as sugars, around the plant. But it also uses energy for other things.

a Study the pictures below and suggest ways in which plants use the rest of this energy.

Getting energy out of food

Plants make their own food by photosynthesis. Plants need light for photosynthesis, so they only make food during the day. But plants need energy day and night.

Respiration is a reaction between glucose and oxygen. The reaction releases energy, which the plant uses. Respiration is the way all living things get energy from their food.

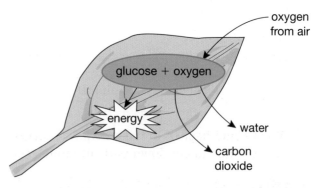

During the day plants use some of the glucose made in photosynthesis immediately. At night plants can't photosynthesise, so they have to use their stores of food. Plants store their food as starch.

- Stored starch is broken down into glucose.
- The glucose is combined with oxygen.
- Energy is released, which the plant can use.
- Carbon dioxide and water are waste products of the reaction.

b Plants release their energy by 'burning' food in oxygen. What is the name of this process?

c What are the waste products?

Photosynthesis and respiration

Plants make food by photosynthesis. They do this only when it is sunny. The waste product of photosynthesis is oxygen.

Plants release energy from their food by respiration. They do this day and night. Plants use oxygen when they respire.

During the day plants photosynthesise and respire. They give out more oxygen than they take in.

At night plants respire but cannot photosynthesise. They give out carbon dioxide.

In photosynthesis plants use carbon dioxide and release oxygen. In respiration it is the other way round. But overall, plants produce more oxygen than they use up.

In fact, without plants there would be no oxygen in the air.

d What could happen to the amount of oxygen in the air if we continue to cut down parts of rainforests?

H **More on photosynthesis and respiration** 🖥 CD-ROM

TASKS

1 a How do all living things obtain the energy they need to live?
   b Write a word equation for this process.

2 In hospital wards, patients often have plants by their bedsides. The nurses always used to remove these plants at night.
   Explain why nurses thought plants were harmless during the day but could be harmful to sick people at night.

1.8 What else do plants need to grow?

All plants make sugars by photosynthesis, but this food is not enough to keep them alive. For example, the plant needs to make chemicals called **proteins** to grow. This is because much of a plant cell is made from proteins.

To make proteins, the plant needs **mineral elements**, such as nitrogen, phosphorus and potassium, which it gets from soil. The minerals are combined with water and are absorbed by the plant's roots.

What minerals do plants need?

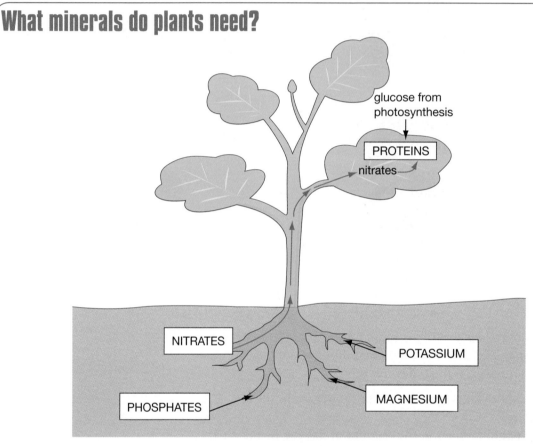

Nitrates are needed to make proteins, which are needed for cell growth.

Phosphates are needed for healthy growth.

Potassium is needed for healthy growth, to flower and produce fruit.

Magnesium is needed to make chlorophyll.

a Why do plants need proteins to live?

b Why do plants need chlorophyll?

c Where do plants get mineral elements like nitrogen, phosphorus and potassium?

Missing mineral

These plants have been grown in solutions. Plant A is healthy because its solution contains all the minerals it needs for healthy growth. The other plants are not as healthy because each of their solutions is missing one important mineral.

- Plant A is healthy. It has all the minerals it needs.
- Plant B lacks nitrates. When a plant lacks nitrates its older leaves are yellow and its growth is stunted.
- Plant C lacks phosphorus. When a plant lacks phosphorus it has yellow leaves and its root growth is stunted.
- Plant D lacks potassium. Plants lacking potassium have yellow leaves with dead areas on them.
- Plant E lacks magnesium. Plants lacking magnesium have very pale leaves.

TASKS

1 For each of the following plants, which mineral do you think is lacking?
   a The plant does not flower. Parts of its leaves are dead.
   b The plant has poor root growth.
   c The plant has yellow leaves and very poor growth.
   d The plant has very pale leaves.

2 What would happen if you grew a crop in the same field, year after year?

3 Hydroponics
   Portfolio Unit 3

Diffusion

Holly sprays herself with perfume in a crowded room. Within a minute, everybody in the room can smell her perfume.

The perfume molecules all start off in a corner of the room. They are moving all the time in different directions. Because of this, after a minute, they have spread throughout the room.

This movement of molecules is called **diffusion**. Molecules move from where they are in high concentration, to where they are in a lower concentration.

a What is diffusion?

Diffusion is very important for green plants. It is how gases like carbon dioxide and oxygen move in and out of the plant.

Moving gases in plants

The diagram shows a cross-section of a leaf. The leaf is made of cells. Gases move between these cells by diffusion.

Plants need carbon dioxide to photosynthesise. But how does a cell deep inside a plant get carbon dioxide? The diagram on the next page shows how.

b After carbon dioxide has passed from the leaf spaces to the leaf cell, more carbon dioxide enters the leaf. Why does this happen?

Molecules of carbon dioxide pass from cell to cell. They move from a cell with a greater concentration of carbon dioxide to one with a lower concentration. This is another example of diffusion.

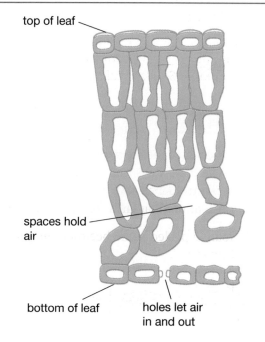

top of leaf

spaces hold air

bottom of leaf

holes let air in and out

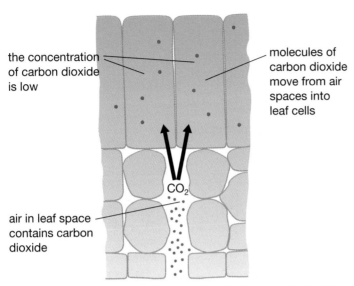

the concentration of carbon dioxide is low

molecules of carbon dioxide move from air spaces into leaf cells

CO_2

air in leaf space contains carbon dioxide

The leaf space holds air. Because it is used up in photosynthesis, the concentration of carbon dioxide in the cell is low.

Diffusion therefore moves carbon dioxide molecules from the air outside the plant to cells deep inside the plant.

Plant cells produce oxygen when they photosynthesise. The concentration of oxygen in cells in the plant is greater than the concentration of oxygen in the air around the plant. The oxygen molecules move by diffusion from the plant cells to the air outside.

c When do plants give off oxygen?

Plants need oxygen for respiration. They also need to get rid of carbon dioxide when they respire. These gases move in and out of the plant by diffusion.

d During respiration, which gas moves into the plant and which gas moves out of the plant?

Water vapour is a gas. Plants contain a lot of water. The concentration of water within a plant is much greater than in the air around. So plant cells lose water by diffusion of water vapour.

TASKS

1 Draw and label two diagrams of a leaf, showing the exchange of gases during respiration. Look at the diagrams for diffusion in photosynthesis to see how to start.

2 Joanne peeled some beetroot and put them into a saucepan of water. Explain why the water turned red.

More questions CD-ROM

We've seen how plants lose water vapour through their leaves. This water needs to be replaced. Plants get the water from the soil. The water moves from the soil into the roots and then up the plant. This happens by diffusion. But there is a special name for diffusion of water through a membrane. It is called **osmosis**.

a What is the special name for diffusion of water through a membrane?

From root to leaf

The cells on the outside of **root hairs** only allow molecules of water and a few other chemicals to pass through. Their cell membranes are called **partially permeable membranes**, because only small molecules can pass through them. The concentration of water in the root hair is less than in the soil, so water passes from the soil into the root hair.

b Why are plant cell membranes called partially permeable membranes?

c Why does water move from the soil into the root?

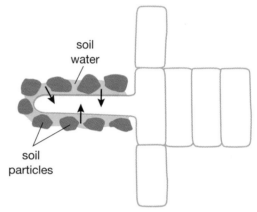

The concentration of water is higher in the soil than in the root hair cell. Water moves into the root hair cell by osmosis.

Once the water is in the plant, osmosis moves it around inside the plant too.

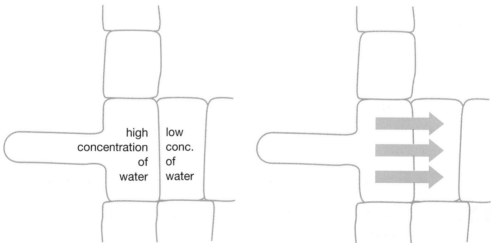

The root hair cell has absorbed water. The concentration of water is now higher in the root hair cell than in the cell next to it. Water passes to the next cell by osmosis.

This process happens all across the root of the plant. It also transfers water from cell to cell in the leaf.

H **More on diffusion and osmosis** CD-ROM

TASKS

1 Joanne cut three cylinders of potato. She put one each into three test tubes.

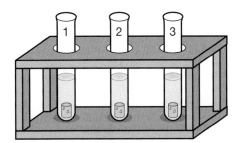

Test tube 1 Strong sugar solution.
Test tube 2 Weak sugar solution.
Test tube 3 Distilled water.

After 30 minutes, she removed the cylinders and weighed each of them. The results were:

Cylinder of potato in test tube	Change in weight
1	lost weight
2	no change in weight
3	gained in weight

Explain the results of this experiment.

2 Joanne then did an experiment with some visking tubing. Visking tubing is made from cellophane and is a partially permeable membrane.

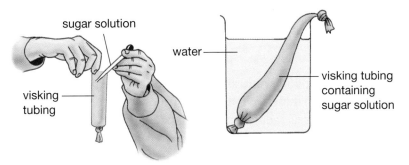

sugar solution

water

visking tubing

visking tubing containing sugar solution

Joanne placed some sugar solution into a piece of visking tubing and sealed the end.

She put the visking tubing into a beaker of water and left it for an hour.
Describe what you think happened.

More questions CD-ROM

1.11 Getting the best out of plants

Neil grows plants for sale in his greenhouse.

Neil wants large, healthy plants. His plants must therefore get the right conditions they need to grow. His plants must also be disease-free.

What is being checked in this greenhouse photo?

What plants need

Plants make their food by photosynthesis. Because they use some of this food for growth, the more a plant photosynthesises, the more it grows. Photosynthesis requires carbon dioxide, water, light and the chlorophyll in the plant's leaves.

The plant's environment must therefore be light and have a supply of carbon dioxide for the plant to make its own food. So, the chemical reaction of photosynthesis can be increased by providing

- more carbon dioxide
- more light
- a higher temperature.

Plants also need a continuous supply of water and minerals if they are to grow well.

a What conditions are necessary for a plant to grow well?

Using a greenhouse

Growers like Neil monitor the conditions in their greenhouses. If Neil knows that certain things are in short supply, he can try to control them. In a greenhouse, conditions are fairly easy to control.

b Look at these pictures of Neil's greenhouse. What condition is being controlled in each case?

Limiting factors CD-ROM

TASKS

1 a Write down the word equation for photosynthesis.
  b Explain why providing a plant with more light and more carbon dioxide makes the plant photosynthesise more.

2 Neil fits an automatic sprinkler system in his greenhouse. This waters the plants as soon as the soil starts to become dry. Why does this help to increase the growth of his plants?

3 Some gardeners light small controlled fires in their greenhouses. How does this help the plants to grow?

More questions CD-ROM

Farmer Stone grows barley for a brewery. To make a profit, she must get a high yield of grain.

Like all plants, barley plants remove nitrates from the field. The plants need the nitrates for healthy growth. A good crop of barley one year will remove most of the nitrates from the soil. The barley plants also take other minerals that they need from the soil.

a **What other minerals might barley plants remove from the soil?**

Farmer Stone has to put these minerals back if she is to get a good yield the following year. This means she will have to add a **fertiliser** to her field.

There are two kinds of fertiliser: artificial and organic. Farmer Stone must understand the advantages and disadvantages of each kind before choosing which one to use on her field.

b **Why do farmers need to put fertiliser on their fields?**

Artificial fertilisers

Artificial fertilisers are made in large chemical factories. Most are very soluble in water. They quickly replace the minerals that crops remove from the soil. A farmer using artificial fertilisers will have a good crop that grows quickly. Spread 3.10 on pages 114 and 115 gives more details.

The **yield** of a grain crop is the amount of grain produced. The farmer using artificial fertilisers will be able to grow huge areas of crops and get a very high yield. This is an example of **intensive farming**.

c **What is the main advantage of artificial fertilisers?**

Artificial fertilisers have disadvantages. They can damage the environment.

1 Farmer Stone applies large quantities of artificial fertiliser to her field.

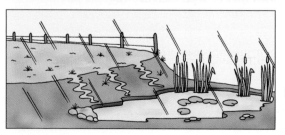

2 When it rains, some of the fertiliser is washed into the pond. When water gets enriched with mineral nutrients, we call this **eutrophication**.

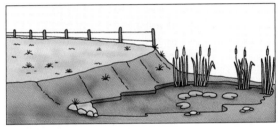

3 Water plants called algae use the minerals to grow. The algae prevent the sunlight from reaching plants lower down in the pond.

4 The plants die and decompose. The decomposition uses a lot of oxygen from the water. Pond life dies.

d How do fertilisers such as nitrates get into ponds, rivers and lakes?

e Why do microscopic algae increase in number?

f Why do fish in the pond die?

Water containing nitrates is also harmful to humans. It may cause cancer.

Organic fertilisers

Manure and seaweed are organic, or natural fertilisers.

Organic fertilisers are much better for the environment than artificial fertilisers. They release their nutrients into the soil more slowly. They also improve the soil texture. If they are washed into lakes or rivers, less damage is done to the environment.

g What are the advantages of organic fertilisers?

Organic farming is different from intensive farming. Crops grown using organic fertilisers do not grow as quickly. They also have a lower yield.

TASKS

1 a Give one example of an artificial fertiliser and one example of an organic fertiliser.
   b Give one advantage and one disadvantage of artificial fertilisers.
   c Give one advantage and one disadvantage of organic fertilisers.

2 a What is eutrophication? Give a reason why it is harmful to:
   • water life
   • humans.
   b Give two ways in which a farmer can reduce eutrophication.

3 Explain why plants grown with organic fertiliser grow well throughout the year.

4 Monitoring the growth of plants to investigate the effect of fertilisers
   Portfolio Unit 3

What is a pest?

A **pest** is something that is harmful to us, or harmful to the food we eat. Pests destroy about 30% of the world's food production. Pests can be insects, weeds, fungi, rodents, etc.

There are lots of insect pests, such as greenfly and the caterpillars of moths, flies and beetles. But not all insects are pests. The ladybird eats greenfly, which eat the leaves of plants.

a What types of insects eat crops?

Weeds growing in a wheat field are pests.

This locust is eating a crop.

The weeds **compete** with the crop for moisture, space, nutrients and sunlight. Plants need all these things for photosynthesis and healthy growth. Competition between weeds and crop plants will therefore seriously reduce the yield from the crop.

b Explain how the lack of sunlight will affect the growth of the crop plants.

In Britain, farmers lose millions of pounds each year from the effects of fungi.

c Which type of fungi can you eat?

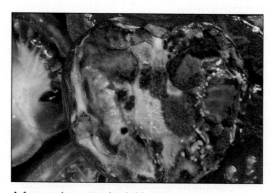

A fungus has attacked this tomato crop.

The Great Famine in Ireland

A fungus causes potato blight. This brought about The Great Famine in Ireland in the 1840s. The famine killed over one million people.

People thought that potato blight was caused by dampness. There was no cure for this disease.

A botanist named Miles Berkely was the first person to suggest that a fungus caused the potato blight. He went on to show that it spread during warm damp weather.

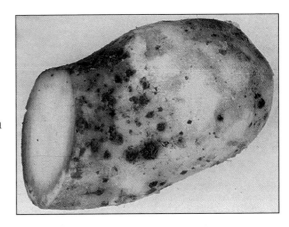

d Suggest why the Irish farmers thought potato blight was caused by dampness.

The diagram shows some of the other pests that can attack potato plants.

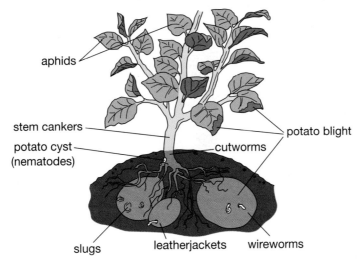

e Find out which of these pests are insects.

Wheat is affected by a fungus called bunt. Fungi spread by producing spores. The spores of the bunt fungus grow filaments (like tiny roots) which break into the wheat plants.

TASKS

1 a List four different types of pests that can affect crop plants.
  b Describe how they affect the crop plants.

2 Explain why farmers do not want to kill all the insects on their crops.

3 Farmers in Ireland now grow several different types of potatoes and other crops. Suggest how this might help to reduce the risk of another famine in Ireland.

 **More questions**

Types of pesticides

The aeroplane in the photograph is spraying **insecticide**. Insecticides are chemicals that are used to kill insect pests.

a Explain how using insecticide helps to increase crop yield.

Some insects are useful for the plants.

b Suggest some ways in which insects can be useful to plants.

Herbicides kill weeds. The farmer does not want his crop killed, so he uses a selective weed killer. This type of weed killer kills all broad-leaved plants, like weeds, but not the narrow-leaved plants being grown, so it kills all the weeds but not the crop.

c Not all crops have narrow leaves. Suggest what might happen if this weed killer is carried by the wind into another field where the crop has broad leaves.

d Explain why it is an advantage for the farmer to get rid of weeds from his crop.

Some seeds are coated with a **fungicide**. This protects the seeds from fungal spores. It also protects the seeds while they are in the soil and as germination takes place.

Fungicides will be sprayed over the crops again as they grow.

Fungicide is used again after crops have been harvested while they are being stored.

You saw in spread 1.12 that using artificial fertilisers is an example of intensive farming. Using pesticides, herbicides and fungicides is another example of intensive farming because they help farmers get the highest yield of crops from their land.

We need protection from microorganisms to stay healthy. Crops need protection too.

Farmers use **pesticides** to help them produce high yields of healthy crops. They must apply all pesticides with great care. They need to wear protective clothing because many of these chemicals are toxic.

Chemicals used for pesticides are carefully tested before they are sold. This is to make sure people and wildlife are not in danger.

Spreading insecticides like this will kill all the insects in the field.

Pesticides in water

In the early 1950s some insecticides contained a dangerous chemical called DDT. This chemical was very successful in killing mosquitoes that were spreading the deadly disease malaria. DDT also kills various crop pests, but it does not break down easily. It stays in the environment for a long time.

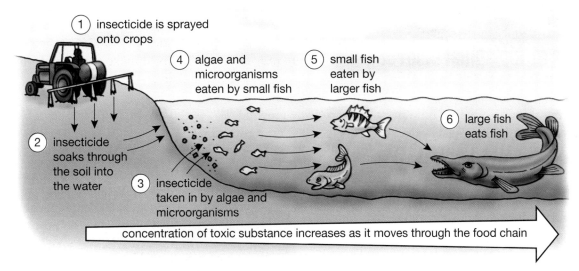

1. insecticide is sprayed onto crops
4. algae and microorganisms eaten by small fish
5. small fish eaten by larger fish
6. large fish eats fish
2. insecticide soaks through the soil into the water
3. insecticide taken in by algae and microorganisms

concentration of toxic substance increases as it moves through the food chain

Many farmers used these insecticides. The chemicals soon washed into the rivers and lakes. The DDT was first taken up by the plants. The small fish fed on the plants. So the level of DDT built up in their bodies. Larger fish ate lots of smaller fish. As the DDT passed along the food chain it became more concentrated at each stage.

e Explain why the large fish died from DDT poisoning, but the small fish did not.

Pesticides containing DDT are now banned from most countries.

TASKS

1. One of the problems farmers have when spraying crops is that the spray can be blown onto another field. Explain why this might be a problem for the farmer and local wildlife.

2. Describe how the following factors can affect crop spraying:
   a amount and direction of wind
   b how close the sprayer is to the edge of the field
   c the pressure of the spray
   d the angle of the spray directed to the crop.

H More questions CD-ROM

1.15 Organic ways of dealing with pests

Some farmers do not like to use chemicals on their land. These farmers are called **organic farmers**. They do not use chemicals to get rid of pests.

a Suggest one reason why organic farmers do not like to use chemical pesticides.

These farmers use living things that will eat the pest or cause a disease in the pest. This method of controlling pests is called **biological control**.

Types of biological control

There are many different types of biological control.

Farmers can help to reduce both pests and weeds by growing different crops in their fields each year. This is called **crop rotation**.

Predator insects are bred in large numbers, then used to control pests.

Plant lice (aphids) are damaging trees in Holland. Ladybirds have been imported from California, where they have been specially bred. The ladybirds are set free into the Dutch countryside to kill the aphids, as shown in the photo.

This method of pest control can take longer to work. However, biological control kills without polluting the environment.

Farmers have to be careful to choose the correct predator insect.

A ladybird eating an aphid.

b Explain why the choice of predator insect is important.

Other examples of biological control are:
- lacewing insects to control greenhouse pests
- bacteria and fungi to control pests such as corn borer and canker worm
- selectively breeding new varieties of crops that are more resistant to pests.

c Why is biological control of pests in greenhouses always more effective than biological control outside in fields?

Removing weeds without herbicides

Organic farmers do not like to use herbicides to get rid of weeds.

d Explain why weeds are a problem for farmers.

Removing weeds by hand is difficult and takes a lot of time.

Machines are being developed to help control weeds. A tractor attachment removes weeds from between the rows of crops.

Removing weeds from within the rows of crops is more difficult. This machine is being developed to recognise crop plants. This will enable it to remove only weeds, leaving the crop plants alone.

These machines can be used on crops that grow in rows such as corn, oil-seed rape, sugar beet and vegetables.

e Suggest the difficulties of developing a machine to remove weeds from crops that do not grow in rows, such as wheat and barley.

TASKS

1 Predator insects can be bought as insect eggs or pupae. They can be put onto crops or garden plants wherever they are needed.
   Suggest why predator insects are sold as insect eggs or pupae.

2 Describe some of the difficulties of using predator insects to protect crops growing in fields.

3 Give two advantages and two disadvantages of using biological control to get rid of pests and weeds.

More questions

Depending on each other

All animals, plants and microorganisms on the planet interact with each other in some way. Animals provide the carbon dioxide that plants need for photosynthesis. And plants provide the oxygen that animals use for respiration.

a What process in plants produces oxygen?

But most of all, animals, plants and microorganisms depend on each other for food. Many animals eat plants. Then other animals eat the animals that have eaten the plants. Microorganisms often feed on dead or living animals and plants.

Food webs

Scientists show which organisms feed on each other using types of flow charts called **food chains** and **food webs**. In any food chain there is a limit to the number of organisms present. This is because some energy is lost as food moves from one energy level to the next.

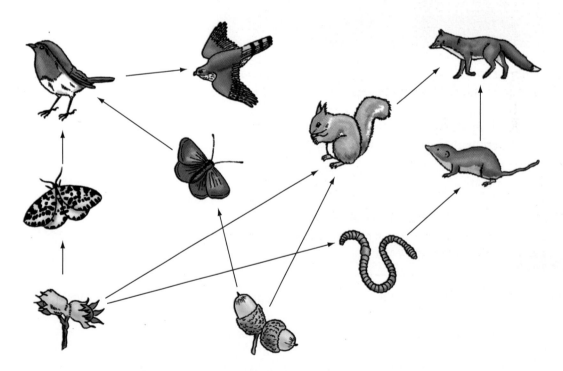

The food web in a woodland. The arrows show the direction in which energy moves.

b What types of animals eat oak leaves?

c Draw a food chain showing how food moves from hazel leaves to the sparrowhawk.

Organisms also have a close relationship with their environment. They can only live successfully where conditions are suitable. Any animal or plant that is living successfully in a habitat is **adapted** to its environment.

The red squirrel is adapted to live in trees. It feeds mostly on pine seeds, hazelnuts, beech nuts and acorns.

The red squirrel's home is called a drey. It constructs the drey in the fork of a tree from twigs, moss, grass and fur.

More on food webs

TASKS

1 Using the woodland food web on the previous page, write down the types of food eaten by robins.

2 Draw a food web for a different type of habitat, like a pond.

3 What is the habitat of the red squirrel? How is the red squirrel adapted to live there?

1.17 The changing environment

All successful organisms are adapted to their environment. But the environment is changing. It's been changing for billions of years, but in the past fifty years the change has been more rapid. The environment is affected by farming, house building and our demand for energy. As we burn more fossil fuels, levels of carbon dioxide in the air are increasing. (See pages 150–151.)

This increase in carbon dioxide levels causes **global warming**. Global warming means we'll have higher temperatures. But as well as higher temperatures, we'll also have more erratic weather, with storms, and periods of very wet or very dry weather.

The glacier in 1928.

The glacier in 2004.

In Argentina, the Upsala Glacier is shrinking by 200 m a year.

These climate changes are affecting the lives of plants and animals. In British woodlands in the spring, oak trees are coming into leaf ten days earlier than they did 30 years ago. In the 1960s, hazel trees produced flowers – called catkins – in February. Today, you can see catkins as early as mid-December! Woodland birds are nesting one week to three weeks earlier than they did 25 years ago. And scientists in Canada have found that squirrels are breeding 18 days earlier than they did just ten years ago. But these changes may not be for the better.

Heavy rains during the nesting season will seriously affect chicks of birds such as the song thrush.

These rapid changes will also seriously affect food webs. Life cycles of plants and animals have to be timed carefully so that food and shelter are available at the right time of the year. If these change, animals could starve. And scientists also think that many plants, including our woodland trees, will be unable to cope with several long, dry summers.

a What might happen to our woodlands in the future because of global warming?

b What will be the effect on animal species that live in the woodland?

H More on the changing environment CD-ROM

TASKS

1 Make a list of factors that are changing the environment in the UK.

2 Different organisms are affected by global warming in different ways.
   a What will happen to organisms in a food web if butterfly caterpillars hatch from eggs before their foodplants are in leaf?
   b Scientists record where different types of butterfly are seen across the UK. In recent years, the purple hairstreak butterfly has been expanding its habitats northwards. Suggest why this is happening.

Intensive farming means trying to produce as much food as possible. This increase in production is achieved by making the best possible use of the land and the animals.

For animals to grow well they need the right sort of food. They also need to be kept warm.

For animals to grow as fast as possible they need to be kept in controlled environments.

The hens in this photograph move freely around the farm to find food. They are called **free range hens**. They use a lot of energy moving around and keeping warm, so they produce fewer eggs.

a Suggest some of the problems of keeping hens like this for egg production.

Examples of intensive farming

These hens live in a battery cage system. A unit like this may have as many as 100 000 birds. These units are large windowless buildings. The light, heat and ventilation are all carefully controlled. The birds are fed a special diet and each bird must have a minimum amount of space.
Machines are used for feeding, cleaning, watering and egg collection.

b Explain why these birds produce more eggs.

c List the extra costs of keeping hens in battery units rather than free range.

Chickens are also bred for food. They grow more quickly in units like this.

Cattle, pigs and sheep can also be kept in special units. The intensive production of cattle, pigs and hens has reduced the cost of producing meat and eggs.

Battery hens.

Why does intensive production work?

These animals grow quicker because:
- they have a high protein diet with additives
- they cannot move around much
- antibiotics are used to reduce the spread of disease
- they are kept warm
- they are safe from predators.

Fish are also intensively farmed. Trout and salmon are kept in specially made pools or in large cages.

> **d** Suggest what sort of conditions are controlled to make sure the fish grow as fast as possible.

The uneaten food and wastes from the fish cause pollution, leading to eutrophication (see pages 26–27).

Some people feel that keeping animals indoors is unnatural and bad for the animals. The welfare of farm animals is studied by farming organisations and the government. Codes of practice have been drawn up by the Farm Animals Welfare Council.

More on intensive farming CD-ROM

TASKS

1 Explain why free range eggs are more expensive than eggs from battery hens.

2 Many people have strong views about animal welfare in intensive systems.
   What do you think are the advantages and disadvantages of intensive farming for:
   a the animals
   b the consumer?

3 Imagine you are a pig farmer.
   State whether you would be an organic pig farmer or an intensive pig farmer.
   Give reasons for your answer.

More questions CD-ROM

Individual organisms that reproduce sexually are all different. Sometimes this variation is useful. It has enabled animals and plants to survive during periods of disease. Without variation, humans may not have survived epidemics of plague and influenza that have swept across the world.

Natural variation has also enabled humans to change the characteristics of other animals and plants.

Animals and plants can be altered over a long period of time by selective breeding. Beef cattle have been bred over centuries to produce more meat.

Before: This is how beef cattle used to look hundreds of years ago.

After: This is how some beef cattle look today.

For thousands of years farmers and gardeners have bred plants and animals to improve their usefulness. These plants and animals have been selectively bred.

a What characteristics have been bred into the sheep and the cereal?

The **selective breeding** process takes many years.
Here is the way a farmer might breed pigs that produce more meat

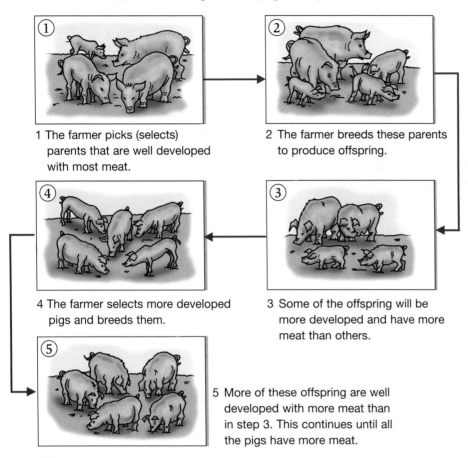

1 The farmer picks (selects) parents that are well developed with most meat.

2 The farmer breeds these parents to produce offspring.

4 The farmer selects more developed pigs and breeds them.

3 Some of the offspring will be more developed and have more meat than others.

5 More of these offspring are well developed with more meat than in step 3. This continues until all the pigs have more meat.

b Why does the farmer keep selecting the pigs that are well developed with more meat?

c Why is this process called selective breeding?

H More on selective breeding, natural selection and evolution CD-ROM

TASKS

1 Scientists want to breed rice which produces a lot of grain and doesn't break easily in the wind when it's growing.

  a What type of head and stem would they want in their selectively bred rice?
  b What steps should they take to do this?
  Portfolio Unit 3 d1

2 **Dairyfarming**
  Portfolio Unit 3  CD-ROM

H More questions CD-ROM

You have seen how animals can be selectively bred. Plants can also be selectively bred. Wild cabbages with certain characteristics were chosen. By breeding them together over many generations, broccoli was developed.

All of these vegetables have been developed from the wild cabbage.

The wild cabbage.

a Describe how our modern-day vegetables are more useful than the original wild cabbage.

Combining traits

We can also breed plants and animals across varieties. We can breed together breeds of animal or varieties of plant with characteristics we want.

This is called **cross-breeding**. It is selective breeding across varieties or breeds.

b Think of your favourite fruits or vegetables. Suggest how you could cross-breed these to improve them.

Farmer John has two breeds of sheep. Breed A produce lots of meat. Breed B have thick fleeces and produce lots of wool. He decides to take parent sheep from breed A and parent sheep from breed B and breed them together.

The offspring of these sheep would have some of the characteristics of breed A and some of breed B. Perhaps some of the offspring would produce as much wool as breed B and as much meat as breed A. That would be very useful for Farmer John, who sells the meat and wool from the sheep.

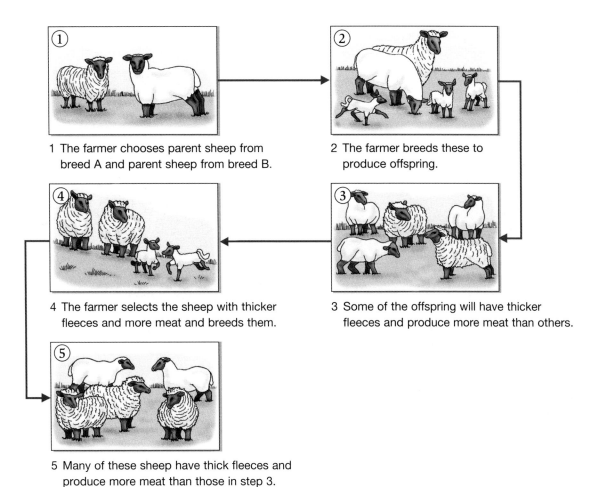

1 The farmer chooses parent sheep from breed A and parent sheep from breed B.

2 The farmer breeds these to produce offspring.

4 The farmer selects the sheep with thicker fleeces and more meat and breeds them.

3 Some of the offspring will have thicker fleeces and produce more meat than others.

5 Many of these sheep have thick fleeces and produce more meat than those in step 3.

c Describe the cross-breeding process a farmer would attempt with the following chickens:
breed A – chickens with plenty of meat
breed B – chickens that lay plenty of eggs.

TASKS

1 Joe's farm is on a small Scottish island. The weather is often cold, wet and windy. List some of the characteristics that Joe needs to selectively breed into his plants to ensure maximum yield.

2 Draw a series of cartoon pictures to show how the process of cross-breeding is carried out.

3 The tomato plants of many years ago produced very few, small tomatoes, of a pale red colour and very little taste.
Describe the improvements that cross-breeding has made to tomato plants.

H More questions CD-ROM

When farmers breed animals, the young animals (offspring) have **features** similar to their parents.

a Which features have been passed on from the parent cow to the young calf?

The instructions for these features are carried on tiny threads called **chromosomes**. Chromosomes are found inside the **nucleus** of every cell.

Each breed of animal and plant has its own number of chromosomes.

We humans have 46 chromosomes inside the nucleus of each and every one of our body cells.

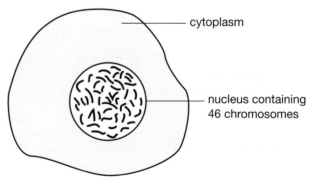

cytoplasm

nucleus containing 46 chromosomes

On the chromosomes are special chemicals called **genes**. These genes carry the instructions for your features, such as:

- hair colour
- eye colour
- shape of ears.

This photograph shows chromosomes that have been put into matched pairs.

One of the chromosomes in each of the pairs has come from the mother. The other chromosome in each pair has come from the father.

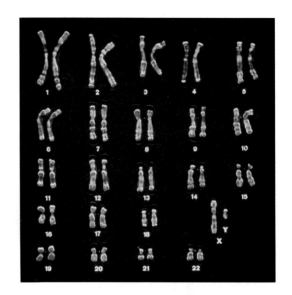

b How many chromosomes have been passed on from the mother?

Egg cells and sperm cells have half the number of chromosomes that other cells in the animal have.

c How many chromosomes do humans have in egg cells and sperm cells?

This is why animals **inherit** characteristics from both their parents. Plants inherit features from their parent plants in the same way.

Animals inherit an **allele** from each parent. The two alleles together form a gene pair.

TASKS

1 Cats have 38 chromosomes inside the nucleus of their body cells.
How many chromosomes will cats have inside the nucleus of their:
a sperm cells
b muscle cells
c egg cells?

2 Suggest some inherited features a farmer would find useful in his:
a sheep
b cows.

3 A plant has 14 chromosomes inside the nucleus of its cells.
How many chromosomes will it have inside the nucleus of its:
a pollen cells (these are sex cells)
b root cells?

4 Suggest some features a farmer would find useful in his fields of corn and potatoes.

Each feature inherited by a plant or animal depends on which alleles are inherited from the mother and father.

All of the sheep in a flock are white. Most of the lambs born are white but from time to time a black lamb is born.

The colour of a lamb's fleece depends on the alleles the lamb inherits from its parents.

Dominant and recessive alleles

Alleles can be either dominant or recessive.

Dominant alleles: their features always show

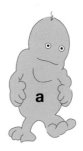

Recessive alleles: their features only show when there are no dominant genes

Let's work out why a black lamb can be born when both its parents are white.

We can use letters to represent the alleles received from the parents:

A is the dominant allele for white fleece.
a is the recessive allele for black fleece.

The different combinations of alleles will produce a different fleece colour:

Aa = white fleece   **Aa** = white fleece   **aa** = black fleece

Mother sheep has a white fleece because she has the dominant allele **A** in her body cells.

Father sheep has a white fleece because he has the dominant allele **A** in his body cells.

The lamb has a black fleece. It gained one **a** allele from each parent so it does not have the dominant gene **A** in its body cells.

The diagram shows all of the possible combinations.

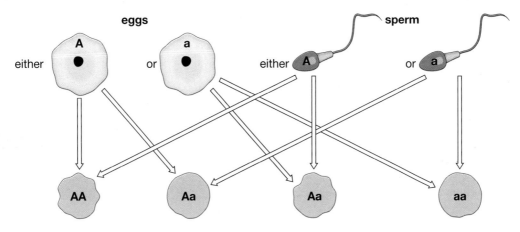

Any lamb born with an **A** allele will have a white fleece. If there is no **A** allele the lamb will have a black fleece.

a Which of the four lambs born will be black? Which will be white?

b From these possible combinations, how many lambs will have a white fleece and how many will have a black fleece?

It is easier to work out the possible combinations of alleles by writing them into a box.

c Work out the possible combinations of fleece colour in lambs from parents with the following:
  i **AA** and **aa**
  ii **AA** and **Aa**
  iii **aa** and **Aa**

		sperm	
		A	a
eggs	A	AA	Aa
	a	Aa	aa

More on genetic inheritance 〔CD-ROM〕

TASKS

1 Joanne has one raspberry bush with thorns and one without thorns. She would like to combine these two bushes to try and grow only bushes without thorns. If **T** is the dominant allele for thorns and **t** is the recessive allele for no thorns, work out the possible combinations.

Joanne thinks the parents carry the allele **TT** (with thorns) and **tt** (without thorns). Describe what Joanne will need to do to have all thornless bushes.

More questions 〔CD-ROM〕

1.23 Genetic engineering

Alex is very interested in **genetic engineering** to improve her herd of pigs.

a   Suggest the type of improvements Alex might want to make to her pigs.

Scientists can take a gene from one animal or plant and put it into the chromosome of a different animal or plant. This is called **gene insertion**.

This process of inserting genes is used in plants and animals to improve certain useful features or give them entirely new ones.

In some countries rice is the main part of people's diet. Many of these people are lacking vitamin A in their diet. This lack of vitamin A causes 500 000 children to go blind every year. A genetically modified form of rice has been developed. This GM rice is called *Golden Rice* because of its orange colour, and it contains vitamin A. This GM crop will improve many lives.

Using a common chemical language

Japanese scientists have successfully inserted a plant gene into pig cells. The pigs contain a gene which changes some of their saturated fat into a type of fat that does not form cholesterol.

b   Explain why this new variety of pigs would be healthier for us to eat than normal pigs.

It is possible to exchange genes from different animals or between plants and animals. This is because chromosomes use a common chemical language.

This language is the same in all living things. It is the same language in roses as it is in horses and humans.

Genetic engineering is used to make insulin. The gene for human insulin production is inserted into the chromosomes of bacteria. The bacteria are grown inside large containers called bioreactors. The bacteria produce insulin which is extracted and purified.

Many drugs are now produced quickly in large quantities by genetic engineering.

The bacteria produce new bacteria that are genetically identical. Each new bacterium is a **clone**.

c   Write down the meaning of the scientific term 'clone'.

Pick and choose

Scientists know which genes are responsible for which features.
Scientists choose which feature they need to improve or add.
They select a plant or animal with the feature they want.

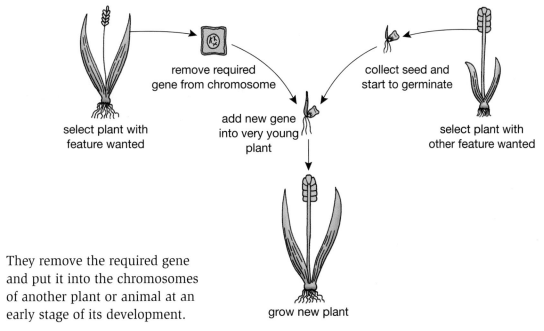

remove required
gene from chromosome

collect seed and
start to germinate

add new gene
into very young
plant

select plant with
feature wanted

select plant with
other feature wanted

grow new plant

They remove the required gene
and put it into the chromosomes
of another plant or animal at an
early stage of its development.

As new cells are formed they all have the improved gene.

d Explain why the new gene needs to be implanted at an
early stage of development.

e Explain why all of the new cells are identical.

More on genetic engineering

TASKS

1 Suggest features of plants that farmers may want to improve by insertion.

2 There is a fish that lives in cold Arctic waters. This fish makes its own type of antifreeze.
Lettuce plants are ruined by frost. It makes the water inside them freeze. Suggest how
scientists may be able to develop a lettuce plant that could grow in winter.

3 Draw a flow diagram to show how gene transfer is carried out.

4 Explain why it is possible to exchange genes from different animals or between plants and animals.

5 **Cloning a plant**
Portfolio Unit 1

More questions

Asif is a crop farmer. He is very happy because genetic engineering in plants has improved his crops.

How might you want to change a crop?

Scientists can put new genes into bacteria, plants and animals. The new genes change the characteristics of these organisms.

Asif is happy with his **genetically modified** (GM) crops because:

- they give a greater yield
- they are disease-resistant
- they can make their own fertilisers
- they grow faster, so they can reach the market early
- they are resistant to weed killers, so Asif can spray the field with weed killer without killing the crop
- they make their own insecticides
- the fruits are tastier and take a long time to go soft and decay.

a Scientists have grown plants with bigger ears of wheat. Explain why this crop would gain more money for Asif.

b Some of Asif's crop plants can make their own fertilisers. Write down **two** advantages of this improvement.

c Why is it an advantage when it takes a longer time for the fruit to go soft?

d Asif can spray his fields of crops with weed killer. Explain how this is an advantage.

e Design a GM crop.
Draw your design. Add labels to your drawing to explain the different characteristics and which plants the genes had been taken from.

Why is genetic modification a concern?

Liz is worried about GM crops.

She does not agree with growing GM crops in our fields.

Liz says: 'WHAT IF . . .'

- ' . . . these supercrops grow too big in too many places and become difficult to control?'
- ' . . . these plants that have their own insecticides kill off too many insects? How will plants pollinate?'
- ' . . . the genes from these plants spread to other plants? The changed characteristics might combine with other plants.'
- ' . . . these new genes are carried in pollen? What will happen when pollen is blown in the wind?'
- ' . . . these genes have an effect on plants in several generations?'

f Write down **two** ways in which insects can be useful to farmers.

g Suggest what would happen if the new genes were to combine with the genes of the weeds in the farmers' fields.

h Some GM plants can make their own weed killer. Suggest what might happen if the pollen from these plants spreads to other fields.

What are the names of some other GM crop designers?

TASKS

1 Explain how each of Asif's changes can increase his profits.

2 Find out about other advantages and disadvantages of genetically modified crops. Prepare a poster showing **your own views**. Support your views with your research.

3 **a** Suggest the problems that might be caused if some GM plants grow too big.
b Explain how this might cause problems for other plants.

More questions CD-ROM

When you or your family have been shopping for fruit and vegetables, have you seen a notice like this in your supermarket or greengrocers?

Organic foods

During the last few years, more and more people have been buying **organic foods**. Organic foods are grown without the use of artificial fertilisers or pesticides, unlike the tomatoes in the photograph which are being sprayed with pesticide.

a Why do you think that some people do not agree with using artificial fertilisers and pesticides?

In your supermarket you might also find pre-packed fruit and vegetables with special 'Organic' labels, like these apples.

Organic foods tend to be produced by small-scale farms.

Organic farming does not use chemicals for fertilisers, pesticides, herbicides or fungicides.

Intensive farming uses these chemicals a lot.

This means more people are needed to work on a farm that produces organic foods.

b **Explain why more people are needed to work on a farm that produces organic foods.**

Organic crop yields are lower than crop yields from intensive farming.

c **Explain why organic foods are often more expensive.**

The organic products that are sold in your supermarket are also guaranteed to contain no genetically modified ingredients. Many people are concerned about the safety of genetically engineered food products. Many others object to these foods on principle. They say genetic engineering involves interfering with nature.

TASKS

1 Here are some of the things people say about organic foods and foods that are produced by intensive farming.

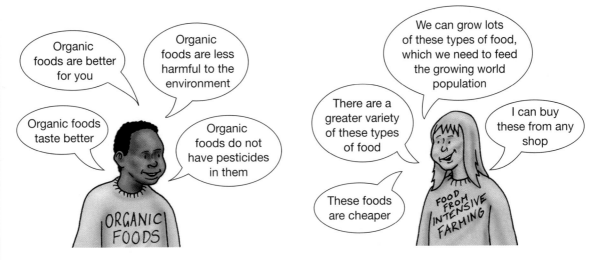

a Which person do you agree with? Explain why.
b If you had to feed a family, would you choose organic foods or foods produced by intensive farming? Explain the reasons for your choice.

2 Describe the ways in which organic farming is different from intensive farming.

Case study: Farming organically at Abbey Home Farm

John Newman is Manager at Abbey Home Farm on the edge of Cirencester. The farm turned organic in 1991. It produces milk, cereals, vegetables, meat and eggs.

The right animals

John says that organic farming is more challenging than intensive farming. He started by choosing the most suitable breeds of animals for the farm. Organically farmed animals can get all the food they need by grazing in fields. They are not fed intensively. John cross-breeds his dairy cows, called Freisians, with beef breeds called Aberdeen Angus and Hereford. The cross-breeds produce top quality beef, but the cows will also produce milk.

Produce is sold at the Organic Farm

The farm also has 500 Lleyn sheep. Like the cattle, they are well-suited to organic farming. They graze on the pasture and don't need much feeding in the winter. They breed well and lamb easily.

The right crops

The farm grows its crops from organic seed, which in the beginning was almost impossible to obtain. Now the farm produces and sells its own organic seed. John uses no fertilisers, only crop rotation, to supply crops with nutrients they need.

For the first part of the crop rotation, particular non-harvest crops like clover are grown in the field because they add nitrogen to the soil. Sheep and cattle grazing on the land add manure to the soil, improving it even more. After two to five years, there are enough nutrients in the soil to grow wheat. After growing other crops like oats, triticale and beans, clover is planted again.

The Lleyn breed of sheep originated from the Lleyn peninsula in North Wales.

Avoiding pests

Pests and diseases can affect the growth of crops. John says that organic farming is more about prevention than cure. The farm has planted 2 km of hedgerow since 1998. John has also left strips of uncultivated land in fields, called 'beetle banks' and 'skylark strips'. These provide food and shelter for birds and insects that eat pests. Because it's organic, the farm is a haven for wildlife. It provides habitats for several rare species of plant, and for birds of prey such as barn owls, buzzards, kestrels and sparrowhawks.

1 Why is the Lleyn breed of sheep a good breed to use on organic farms?

2 Give three reasons why Abbey Home Farm can be described as an organic farm.

3 Explain why birds of prey can be seen on Abbey Home Farm, but are less likely to be seen on intensively farmed land.

1   Scientists use chemicals called catalysts and enzymes in industry.
    a What do catalysts do?   [1]
    b What is an enzyme?   [1]

2   Naomi was given a course of antibiotics for an infection by her doctor.
    a What type of microorganism did the doctor think caused Naomi's infection?   [1]
    b For what type of infection would her doctor not prescribe antibiotics?   [1]
    c When was the first antibiotic discovered?   [1]

3   a Plants make their own food. What is this process called?   [1]
    b Where does this process take place?   [1]
    c What are the products of this process?   [2]
    d What do plants do with the products of photosynthesis?   [2]

4   Joanne placed a potato cylinder in some water in a test tube. What happened:
    a to the water molecules?   [1]
    b to the mass of the potato cylinder, and why?   [2]

5   Plants need minerals for healthy growth.
    a Name **four** minerals needed by plants.   [4]
    b Where do plants get these minerals from?   [1]
    c What part of the plant takes up these minerals?   [1]

6   a Explain why having weeds in a crop will reduce the crop yield.   [2]
    b Describe **one** method of weed control used by organic farmers. [1]
    c Describe **one** method of weed control used by other farmers.   [1]

7   Farmers want to breed plants and animals with useful features.
    Which **two** of these are useful features?

    disease resistance   **leaves damaged by rain**
    produce few eggs   **produce lots of milk**   [2]

8   Here are five sentences about selective breeding. They are in the wrong order.
    Copy out the sentences in the correct order.

    1 Offspring grow and farmers again select those with the best features.
    2 Farmers breed from these parents.
    3 The process is repeated for many years.
    4 Farmers choose the parents with the most useful features.
    5 Farmers decide which features are most useful in the plants or animals.   [4]

9   Chromosomes are found inside all cells. They carry genetic information.
    a Where inside the cells are chromosomes found?   [1]
    b Explain why you have some characteristics inherited from your father and
      some from your mother.   [2]
    c Write down one characteristic that can be inherited.   [1]

10 John has produced some beer by fermentation.

   a Copy and complete the word equation for fermentation:

      glucose → _____ + _____ + energy

                                                       [2]

   b List **four** conditions that yeast needs to carry out fermentation. [4]

11 Helen sets up several fermentations using yeast in conical flasks, as shown in the diagram. She sets up the flasks at different temperatures. She counts the bubbles of gas produced every minute.

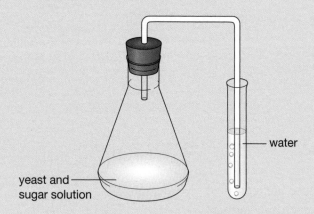

yeast and sugar solution

water

Temperature, °C	Number of bubbles per minute
10	15
20	30
30	55
40	60
50	45
60	0

   a What gas produces the bubbles? [1]

   b What chemical product would you find in the flask at the end of the fermentation? [1]

   c What conclusions would Helen make about the best temperature for fermentation? [2]

   d Why was the fermentation best at this temperature? [2]

12 Food production in microorganisms requires enzymes.

   a In what organisms are these enzymes found for:
- brewing
- baking
- yogurt production? [3]

   b Describe a major difference between the enzymes in the brewing and yogurt industries. [1]

13 Use the words in this list to answer the questions.

   cell wall   chloroplast   cytoplasm
   large vacuole   membrane   nucleus

   a Which parts of a cell are found in both plant cells and animal cells? [3]

   b Which parts of a cell are found in plant cells only? [3]

   c Which part of a cell controls what enters and leaves the cell? [1]

   d In which part of a cell does photosynthesis take place? [1]

14 **a**   Copy and complete the following word equation for photosynthesis:

      _____ + _____ → glucose + _____

                                                     [3]

   b What form of energy is used to power the reaction? [1]

   c What chemical does the plant need to absorb this type of energy? [1]

   d What metal does this chemical contain? [1]

   e In what part of the plant does photosynthesis take place? [1]

   f What happens to the glucose after it is made? [2]

15 This question is about respiration in plants.

   a Write out the equation for plant respiration. [1]

   b How is plant respiration different from animal respiration? [1]

   c Give **three** ways in which a plant uses the energy released during respiration. [3]

   d When during the day does a plant carry out respiration? [1]

16 Neil bought four plants. Three of the four plants were showing signs of mineral nutrient deficiency.

Plant	Stem length, mm	Root length, mm	Appearance
A	300	300	healthy
B	250	100	yellow leaves
C	150	150	pale leaves
D	250	250	very pale leaves

In Neil's gardening book, symptoms of mineral deficiency are listed as:
- lacking nitrogen: pale, very poor growth
- lacking phosphorus: yellow leaves, poor root growth
- lacking magnesium: very pale leaves.

a Which plant was not suffering from a mineral deficiency? [1]

b For the other three plants, suggest what mineral was missing in each case. [3]

17 a What is a chromosome? [1]

b There are chromosomes in every cell. In which part of the cell are chromosomes found? [1]

c In a human, how many chromosomes are there in:

  i a muscle cell [1]

  ii a sperm cell [1]

  iii an egg cell [1]

  iv a fertilised egg cell? [1]

18 Scientists have produced tomatoes that take twice as long to ripen as ordinary ones. The scientists changed the gene that controls the ripening process.

a What is meant by the term **gene**? [2]

b Describe the advantages of a longer ripening tomato. [1]

c Suggest **one** other helpful change that might be made to plants by changing their genes. [1]

d Suggest **one** possible disadvantage that might occur due to changing the genes in plants. [1]

19 a What is cloning? [1]

b Suggest **two** possible advantages of genetic cloning in animals. [2]

c Suggest **two** advantages of producing plants by genetic cloning. [2]

d Suggest **two** disadvantages of producing plants by genetic cloning. [2]

e Explain why it is possible to exchange genes from different plants and animals. [2]

20 Some cattle are bred by **artificial insemination**. This involves collecting sperm from the best bulls and placing the sperm into the best cows.
Joe is a cattle farmer. He has always bred cattle by **selective breeding**. He is considering using the process of artificial insemination because it is quicker.

a Explain why the process of **selective breeding** takes many years to gain the characteristics needed. [4]

b Explain the differences between **selective breeding** and **artificial insemination**. [2]

21 Suggest how genetic engineering might be used to prevent inherited diseases. [4]

22 Suggest **three** advantages of producing insulin by genetic engineering rather than by extracting it from sheep or pigs. [3]

23 Various breeds of dogs have been developed for different purposes.

a Suggest **three** different uses for different breeds of dogs. [3]

b Describe the features that each breed needs to carry out its job. [3]

Case study: Ambulance paramedic

Starting out

Jason is an ambulance paramedic. When Jason was 18 years of age he joined the NHS (National Health Service) Ambulance Service as a Care Assistant. Jason had 4 GCSEs at grade C or above. He needed to pass a series of entrance examinations and a medical examination. Jason has to be physically fit and hold a clean driving licence.

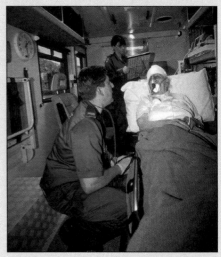

As a Care Assistant Jason was involved with non-emergency work. He transported patients to and from hospital. After two years, Jason became an Ambulance Technician and then an Ambulance Paramedic.

Paramedic crew attending to an elderly patient.

In an emergency

Now Jason is part of the Accident and Emergency Service. His job often requires him to treat people suffering from a cardiac arrest (heart attack).

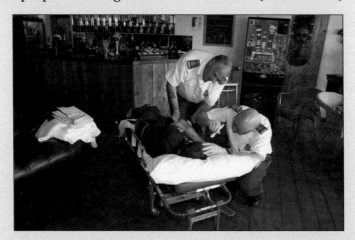

If the patient is unconscious, Jason will check the airway is open. Jason will then check to see if the patient is breathing. If the patient is not breathing, Jason will check for the patient's pulse. If there is no pulse, Jason knows that the heart is no longer beating.

Every time the heart beats it pumps blood around the body. The pulse you feel is the movement of blood through an artery. Arteries carry blood away from the heart. The blood carries food and oxygen around the body to all the cells. The cells use the food and oxygen during respiration. Respiration provides the energy we need for life processes. The blood then returns to the heart through veins.

If the heart is not pumping blood around the body the cells will stop working. Jason needs to carry out CPR (cardio-pulmonary resuscitation) to try and make the heart start pumping blood again. Jason also uses heart defibrillators to try and make the heart beat again. The patient is then taken to the hospital.

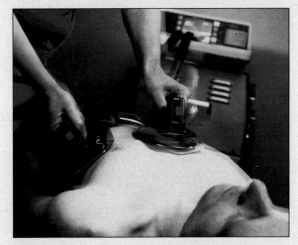

Man receiving emergency defibrillation.

1 Describe the different jobs carried out by:
   a arteries
   b veins.

2 If Jason cannot feel a pulse he knows the heart is not beating. Explain why.

3 If Jason cannot start the heart beating again the patient will die. Explain why.

How this chapter can help you with your portfolio

Unit 1 CD-ROM

You can learn about your pulse rate and what happens to your body when you exercise, which will help you with these portfolio tasks:

● Using microorganisms safely in the laboratory

● Using aseptic technique to test water for contamination by bacteria

● Investigating the effect of disinfectants on the growth of bacteria

● Investigating the effect of different antibiotics on the growth of bacteria

● The forensic detection of glucose

● The forensic detection of alcohol

Unit 3 CD-ROM

This chapter will also help you with these portfolio tasks:

● Monitoring the effects of physical activity on the human body

2.1 Why do we breathe faster and harder?

Bill needs to check Tara's **breathing rate**, at rest and after exercise.

One way to measure breathing rate is to count the rise and fall of your rib cage.

a As your rib cage rises are you breathing in or out?

A more accurate way to measure breathing rate is to use a spirometer.

The photograph shows Tara using a spirometer.

The spirometer prints out a pattern of Tara's breathing.

b Copy the spirometer trace into your book.
On the trace label the part where:

- Tara is resting
- Tara is exercising.

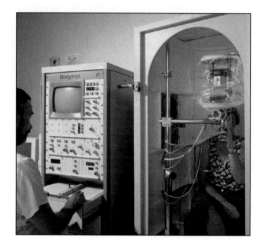

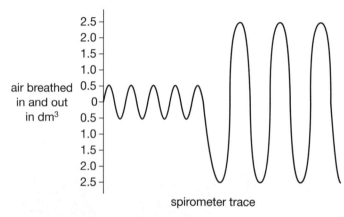

air breathed in and out in dm³

spirometer trace

How exercise affects breathing

As Tara exercises, her breathing rate increases. Tara needs more energy in her muscle cells for the exercise she is doing.

To produce more energy Tara needs more oxygen and more glucose. The oxygen and glucose react together inside Tara's cells to produce more energy. This reaction is called **aerobic respiration**.

We can show aerobic respiration as a word equation:

oxygen + glucose → carbon dioxide + water + energy

'Aerobic' means that oxygen is used up. As Tara exercises she needs more oxygen, so her breathing rate increases.

c Tara's muscle cells will also need glucose for respiration. Where from inside Tara's body does the glucose come from?

Running step-by-step

These pictures and notes explain how Tara's respiration changes as she runs a race.

1 To make more energy, her muscle cells need more oxygen and glucose.

2 Tara breathes faster and harder. Her **pulse rate** increases to deliver oxygen to her muscles more quickly.

3 Tara cannot breathe fast enough. Respiration is now taking place without oxygen. This is called **anaerobic respiration**. (You have learnt about anaerobic respiration of yeast in Chapter 1.)

4 Lactic acid is made during anaerobic respiration. Lactic acid is poisonous and in Tara's muscles it causes cramp, so her body needs to get rid of it. Oxygen is needed to break down the lactic acid. The lactic acid will stay in Tara's cells until enough oxygen is breathed in to break it down. This is called **oxygen debt**. Tara will continue to breathe faster and harder until all of the lactic acid has been broken down.

This is the word equation for anaerobic respiration:

glucose → lactic acid + energy

This form of respiration gives off much less energy than aerobic respiration.

 **More on aerobic respiration** CD-ROM

TASKS

1 Tara runs a 100 metre race.
   a Explain why she can run the whole race without breathing.
   b Explain why she is out of breath at the end of the race.

2 Tara runs a marathon.
   a Half way through the marathon Tara suffers with cramp. Explain why.
   b Explain how Tara's body can get rid of this cramp.

3 **Monitoring the effect of physical activity on the human body** CD-ROM
   Portfolio Unit 3

 **More questions** CD-ROM

Tara understands that oxygen travels to her cells in her blood.

She wants to know how the oxygen gets into her blood.

This X-ray shows Tara's rib cage and lungs.

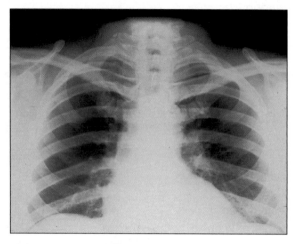

This part of the body is called the **thorax**.

a Use the diagram below to help you work out the names of all the different parts on the X-ray.

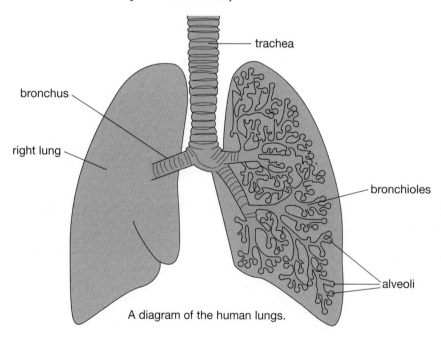

A diagram of the human lungs.

How does oxygen move from Tara's lungs into her blood?

Alveoli and exchanging gases

The air we breathe in moves all the way through the lungs until it reaches the **alveoli**. The oxygen then moves from the alveoli into the blood capillaries.

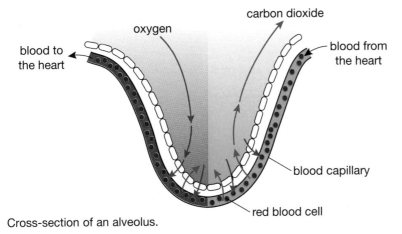

oxygen

carbon dioxide

blood to
the heart

blood from
the heart

blood capillary

red blood cell

Cross-section of an alveolus.

The structure of the alveoli and the capillaries helps the oxygen to move into the blood:

• the walls of the alveoli are only one cell thick
• the insides of the alveoli are moist
• each alveolus has lots of capillaries around it
• the wall of the blood capillary is only one cell thick.

Carbon dioxide is the waste gas from respiration. It needs to be removed from the body. Carbon dioxide is carried from the cells to the lungs in the blood plasma.

When the blood reaches the lungs the carbon dioxide moves from the blood into the alveoli. The carbon dioxide is then breathed out of the lungs.

TASKS

1 Explain how the structure of the lungs and the capillaries helps oxygen to pass into the lungs.

2 Draw a diagram of an alveolus and a blood capillary. Label your diagram and use arrows to show the movement of gases into and out of the lungs.

3 Imagine you are an oxygen molecule. Write a story about your journey through the body. Your story should include these phrases:
• from the air
• through the nose
• into the lungs
• around the body
• used in a cell for respiration
• combined with carbon to form carbon dioxide
• carried back to the lungs
• then passed back out into the air.

 **More questions** CD-ROM

Tara needs to understand how her lungs work so she can control her breathing.

a What happens to your rib cage as you breathe in and out?

Every breath you take

At the bottom of your thorax is a sheet of muscle called the **diaphragm**. This diagram shows how your body makes you breathe in.

1 The *intercostal* muscles between your ribs contract (become shorter).
2 The muscles make your rib cage move upwards and outwards.
3 Your diaphragm moves downwards.
4 There is now more space inside your thorax.
5 The pressure inside your thorax is now lower than the pressure outside your body.
6 This difference in pressure causes air to be drawn into your lungs.

To breathe out the opposite happens.

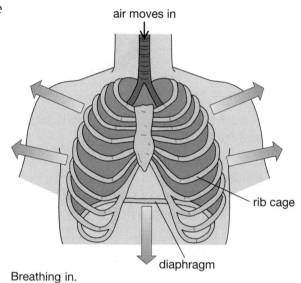

air moves in

rib cage

diaphragm

Breathing in.

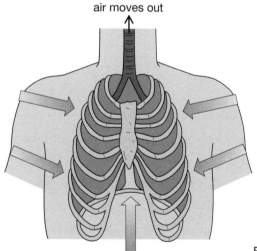

air moves out

Breathing out.

b Describe the six stages that will happen in your body to make you breathe out.

Breathing faster and harder

Bill the trainer can tell how well Tara's lungs are working by measuring the amount and the force of the air breathed out.

Breathing properly depends on the strength of the muscles involved and how much the lungs can stretch.

When Tara is resting, her **breathing rate** is 12 breaths per minute. When Tara is running, her breathing rate increases to 100 breaths per minute.

Tara has to control her breathing. She needs to take frequent, deep breaths to get lots of air into her lungs.

These charts show what is in the air that Tara breathes in and what is in the air she breathes out.

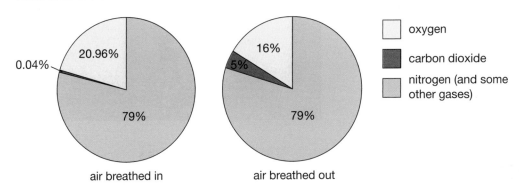

air breathed in   air breathed out

oxygen

carbon dioxide

nitrogen (and some other gases)

c Write down the percentage of oxygen breathed in.

d Write down the percentage of oxygen breathed out.

e Which gas stays the same amount before and after?

f Explain why the air breathed out is warmer and has more moisture than the air breathed in.

H More on breathing in and out   CD-ROM

TASKS

1 Draw a bar chart to show the difference in Tara's breathing rate during rest and during exercise.

2 Find out what you should do if someone stopped breathing.

3 a Draw bar charts to show the percentage of different gases in:
   i the air breathed in
   ii the air breathed out.
  b Use the information in the bar charts to explain why it is possible to revive someone by mouth-to-mouth resuscitation.

4 Finish the table to show what the body does when breathing in and breathing out.

	Intercostal muscles	Rib cage	Diaphragm
Breathing in			
Breathing out			

2.4 Getting the oxygen to cells

Bill the trainer has planned Tara's training programme. Tara is to train high up in the mountains for the last month before the marathon. Tara is surprised by this and asks Bill to explain why.

Red blood cells carry oxygen

Bill explains that oxygen is carried by **red blood cells**. High up in the mountains there is less oxygen in the air. To overcome this problem the body makes more red blood cells.

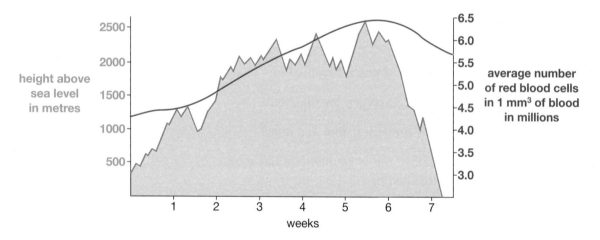

As Tara trains high up in the mountains, her body will make extra red blood cells. When she comes back down to lower levels, the extra red blood cells can carry more oxygen.

> **a** Explain why extra oxygen in her body will help to improve Tara's performance.

Tara is still unsure why oxygen should move from her lungs into her blood. Bill tries to explain.

Oxygen is transferred by diffusion

Oxygen moves from inside the lungs into the blood by diffusion. In spread 1.9 (pages 20 and 21) you saw that gases move from where they are in high concentration to where they are in low concentration. This is how oxygen moves from the lungs into the blood. Oxygen diffuses from the area of higher concentration (the lungs) into the area of lower concentration (the blood).

66

b Explain what is meant by the word 'diffusion'.

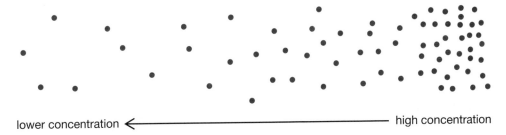

lower concentration ⟵————————————————— high concentration

The oxygen diffuses:

- through the wall of the alveolus
- through the wall of the capillary and into the red blood cell.

Diffusion is also how carbon dioxide moves out of the blood and into the lungs. The concentration of carbon dioxide is higher in the blood capillaries than it is inside the lungs. So carbon dioxide diffuses from the blood into the lungs.

c Explain why there is more carbon dioxide in the blood when it returns to the lungs from the body.

The blood carries the oxygen around the body. When it reaches cells with a low concentration of oxygen inside them, diffusion takes place. Oxygen moves from the blood into the cell, through the semi-permeable membrane.

If there is a high concentration of carbon dioxide inside the cell then diffusion will take place. Carbon dioxide moves out of the cell and into the blood.

TASKS

1 Suggest other areas inside the body where diffusion takes place.

2 Draw a poster to show the diffusion of oxygen from the alveoli into the blood. Use different coloured pens to represent the different molecules. Add labels to your poster.

3 a What is the job of the red blood cells?
   b Explain why the body makes extra red blood cells when a person is staying high up in the mountains.
   c Which part of the blood carries the carbon dioxide?

4 Draw a diagram to show:
   - how oxygen diffuses from the blood into body cells
   - how carbon dioxide moves from the body cells into the blood.

Arteries

Bill the trainer needs to measure Tara's **heart rate**.

Bill can take Tara's pulse to measure her heart rate.

a Can you feel your pulse?

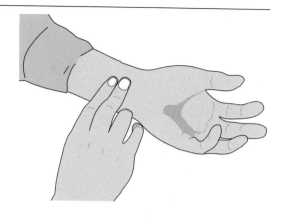

Every time your heart beats it pumps blood around your body. Your **pulse** is the wave of blood that pushes through your **arteries**.

b Calculate how fast your heart is beating.
  • Count your pulse for 30 seconds.
  • Double this figure.
  • This is how fast your heart is beating in one minute. It is called the pulse rate.

The photograph shows a more accurate method of measuring heart rate.

At rest your heart rate will probably be between 60 and 80 beats per minute. During exercise your heart rate could increase up to 110 or 120 beats per minute.

c Explain why your heart needs to beat faster as you exercise. (The answer to this question can be found in spread 2.1.)

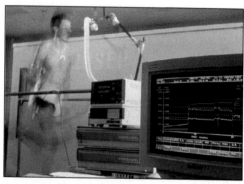

This person is running on a treadmill. This will show how the heart rate increases with exercise.

Tara is still not sure how her blood manages to get to all parts of her body. This flow chart will help to explain.

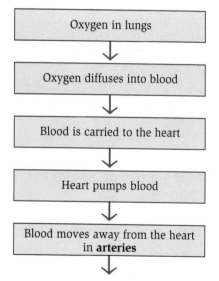

| Oxygen in lungs |
| Oxygen diffuses into blood |
| Blood is carried to the heart |
| Heart pumps blood |
| Blood moves away from the heart in **arteries** |

The blood leaving the heart is travelling very fast and at a high pressure. This means arteries need to have thick, muscular walls.

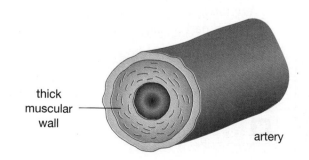

thick muscular wall

artery

Capillaries

To reach every cell in the body, the blood needs
to travel through tiny vessels called **capillaries.**
The capillary wall is only one cell thick so
things can easily pass into and out of the capillaries.

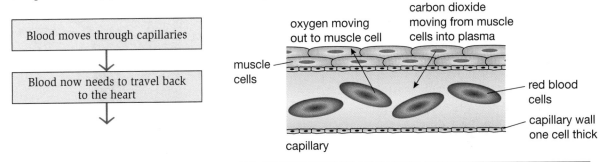

Blood moves through capillaries
↓
Blood now needs to travel back to the heart
↓

oxygen moving out to muscle cell

carbon dioxide moving from muscle cells into plasma

muscle cells

red blood cells

capillary wall one cell thick

capillary

Veins

The blood returning to the heart is travelling
much more slowly and at a lower pressure.
The vessels that carry blood back to the heart
are called **veins**. Veins have thinner walls and
a large inner area so blood flow is not slowed
down. Veins have **valves** to prevent backflow.

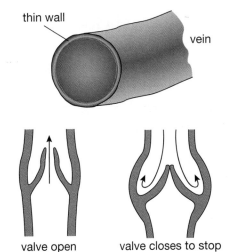

thin wall

vein

Veins carry the blood back to the heart
↓
The heart then pumps the blood back to the lungs
↓
This **circulation** starts all over again

valve open

valve closes to stop backflow of blood

TASKS

1 Draw labelled diagrams of the three types of blood vessels.

2 Copy and complete these sentences:
   a Arteries need to have thick muscular walls because _____.
   b Veins have thinner walls and a large inner area because _____.
   c Capillaries have walls only one cell thick because _____.

3 a Describe the job of the valves.
   b Explain why valves are needed in veins but not in arteries.
   c Where else in the body could we find valves?

More questions CD-ROM

Tara understands that her heart pumps blood all around her body.

This is a photograph of a human heart.

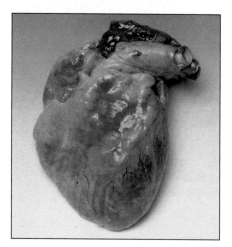

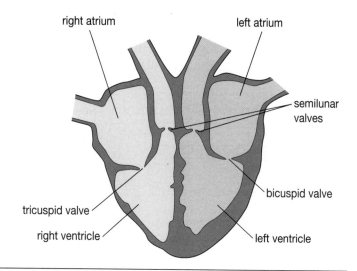

The heart and circulation

Your heart is about the same size as your clenched fist. It is like two separate pumps, placed side by side. The blood from one side does not mix with blood from the other side.

The **left atrium** of your heart receives blood from the lungs.

a What is added to blood as it passes through the lungs?

The blood passes down into the **left ventricle**.

The bicuspid valve closes behind the blood. This stops the blood flowing back into the atrium.

As the left ventricle contracts, the blood is forced out into the aorta. As the blood leaves the left ventricle the semilunar valve closes behind it.

b What is the job done by the valves in the heart?

Blood leaves the heart through the **aorta**.

The blood now travels all around the body delivering oxygen, food and hormones to the cells. It collects carbon dioxide, water and other waste products from the cells.

When the blood returns to the heart, it takes this route through the right side of the heart:

right atrium → tricuspid valve → right ventricle
→ semilunar valve → leaves heart

c Where does the blood go when it leaves the right ventricle?

The left ventricle has a thicker wall than the right ventricle.

d Which ventricle pumps blood further around the body?

As the blood travels around the body it carries oxygen and food that are needed by the cells.

e Explain why cells need oxygen and glucose.

The blood collects carbon dioxide, water and other waste products from the cells. The carbon dioxide is carried back to the heart, then pumped to the lungs.

f What happens to the carbon dioxide when it reaches the lungs?

Blood cells.

Components of blood

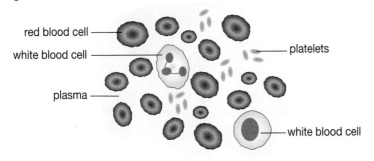

Part of blood	Job
red blood cells	carry oxygen
white blood cells	protect body against infection by eating bacteria and making antibodies
platelets	help blood to clot
plasma	carries dissolved food, hormones, carbon dioxide, water and other waste products

More on the heart CD-ROM

TASKS

1 Describe how the different parts of the blood help to protect us when we cut ourselves.

2 Study the picture of blood.
   a How many types of white blood cells are there?
   b What is the name of the liquid that carries all the blood cells?
   c Which part of the blood is the smallest?

3 Inside the heart there are four valves.
   a What are the names of these valves?
   b What is the function of the valves?

4 Explain why the wall of the left ventricle is thicker than the wall of the right ventricle.

5 Explain why it is important that the blood in the two sides of the heart does not mix together.

More questions CD-ROM

2.7 Why do we go red and sweat?

During the marathon Tara will need to take regular drinks of water.

Tara does not like this idea. She thinks it will slow her down.

Bill the trainer explains that as Tara runs, more respiration takes place in her muscle cells.

a Write down the word equation for aerobic respiration.

Heat energy is released by respiration. Tara will become hotter.

b What is normal body temperature?

As Tara becomes hotter, her skin will become red and she will start to sweat.

Sweat is made up of 99% water. Sweat glands pump sweat onto the skin's surface.

The sweat evaporates. As sweat evaporates it takes heat energy from the body.

c If you put water on the back of your hand, the water evaporates, leaving your hand feeling cold. Explain why your hand feels cold.

Tara now understands why she needs to drink water during the race.

But she still does not understand why her skin goes so red.

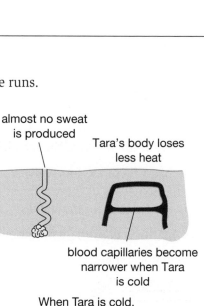

Why the skin goes red

The diagram shows what happens in Tara's skin as she runs.

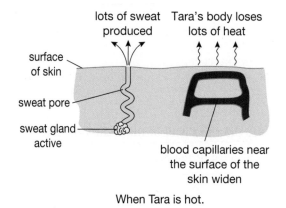

lots of sweat produced · Tara's body loses lots of heat

surface of skin

sweat pore

sweat gland active

blood capillaries near the surface of the skin widen

When Tara is hot.

almost no sweat is produced · Tara's body loses less heat

blood capillaries become narrower when Tara is cold

When Tara is cold.

The blood vessels close to the surface of the skin become wider. More blood is able to flow through these blood vessels. More heat is lost from the blood.

This extra blood flowing near the surface of the skin causes the skin to look red.

Tara's body temperature must be kept at 37°C. It's Tara's nervous system that detects changes in her body temperature. Nerve cells in her body are sensitive to changes in blood and skin temperature. Her brain sends messages along nerves to her blood vessels and to her sweat glands.

After the marathon Tara will feel very cold.

To help to keep her warm her body will:

- start to shiver
- stop sweating
- make her blood vessels become narrow
- make her hairs stand on end.

When we shiver our muscles are using energy, so more respiration has to take place.

d Explain why shivering helps to keep you warm.

 **More on homeostasis and the nervous system** CD-ROM

Find out why the athlete is using such a shiny blanket.

TASKS

1 Explain why you feel cold when you get out of a swimming pool.

2 Draw a diagram (similar to the one above) to show what happens inside your skin when you become too cold. You need to label your diagram.

3 Explain how a space blanket (like the one shown in the photograph above) helps to keep an athlete warm.

 More questions CD-ROM

This is the meal Tara will eat before the marathon. This meal is full of **carbohydrates**.

Foods rich in carbohydrates are cereals, potatoes and pasta.

Tara's body can convert carbohydrates to energy very quickly.

a Why does Tara eat pasta before the marathon?

Tara enjoys pasta meals, but does not understand why they are so important before a marathon.

Food as fuel

Tara needs lots of energy to run the marathon. She gets energy from respiration. So her muscle cells must respire quickly.

The word equation for aerobic respiration is:

oxygen + glucose → carbon dioxide + water + energy

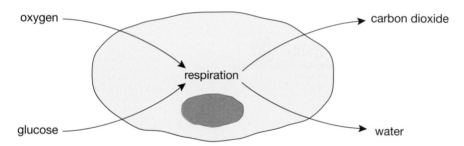

The more energy that is needed, the faster respiration takes place. So more glucose is needed.

Blood needs to reach every cell in your body. Oxygen and glucose have to be delivered to every cell. Carbon dioxide and water have to be removed from every cell.

Tara still does not understand how the glucose in her food gets into her muscle cells.

Absorbing the fuel

As food passes through the mouth and the stomach it is digested (broken down). The **digested** food then moves into the small intestine.

Lots of small food molecules need to pass into the blood. For this to happen the small intestine needs to have a large surface area. The surface area of the small intestine is about 9 square metres. To provide this large surface area the small intestine is:

• 6 metres long
• folded many times.

On the inside of the small intestine there are lots of finger-like projections. These projections are called **villi**.

Villi have:

• thin walls
• a good blood supply.

They also increase the surface area of the small intestine.

This flow chart shows what happens next.

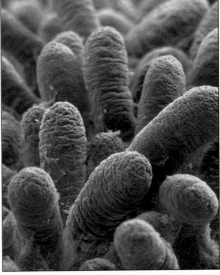

Villi on the inside of the intestine wall.

Glucose and other small food molecules pass through the villi wall into the blood.

↓

The blood carries the glucose to the muscle cells.

↓

There is a higher concentration of glucose in the blood than in the muscle cells.

↓

So glucose can diffuse into the muscle cells.

↓

Glucose is then used in respiration.

TASKS

1 Draw a labelled diagram to show how glucose is absorbed into the blood.

2 Explain why food has to be broken down into small soluble particles.

3 Why is glucose needed by your cells?

4 Write out the word equation for respiration and explain what it means.

5 Some people suffer from coeliac disease. The irritation caused by this disease often destroys the villi in the small intestine. People with coeliac disease have stunted growth. Explain why.

More questions CD-ROM

2.9 Controlling blood sugar

Tara would rather eat sugary food than her pasta meal.

Tara should not eat too many sweet foods because she does not want to put on too much weight.

Pasta and sugar have different types of carbohydrate:

- the carbohydrate in sweet foods is sugar
- the carbohydrate in pasta is starch.

Tara needs to be careful how much sugary food she eats.

Too much of a good thing

In Tara's small intestines, glucose, a product of digestion, diffuses into her blood. There is now too much glucose in Tara's blood.

Tara is not exercising so her muscle cells cannot use all the glucose. Tara's pancreas produces a **hormone** called **insulin**.

A hormone is a chemical messenger. There are many hormones inside your body. They are carried in the blood plasma to all the different parts of your body.

The insulin tells Tara's liver to remove the glucose and save it until her body needs it.

The hormone insulin controls the amount of glucose in Tara's blood.

Some people cannot produce enough of the hormone insulin. They have **diabetes**. If their blood sugar levels are allowed to rise too high they become very ill. Some diabetics are treated with tablets, controlled diet and exercise. Other sufferers of diabetes need to inject with insulin twice a day.

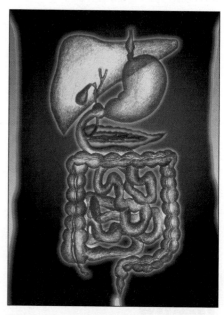

The human digestive system showing the pancreas (highlighted in blue).

a Some people develop diabetes after their pancreas has become damaged. Explain why.

b Explain why it is important for diabetics to control their diet.

c Insulin is a protein. Why can diabetics not swallow insulin tablets rather than have insulin injections?

d Write a list of the organs your body uses to control blood sugar.

Homeostasis

Your body is trying to control things and keep everything constant inside you, such as:

- blood sugar levels
- temperature
- amount of carbon dioxide
- amount of water.

The process by which your body tries to keep all these things constant is called **homeostasis**.

e Why is it important for your body to control the amount of carbon dioxide in your blood?

Our nervous system is also involved in homeostasis. But whereas the nervous system causes rapid changes to our bodies by sending messages along nerves, changes brought about by hormones are much slower. Hormones also control our growth and development.

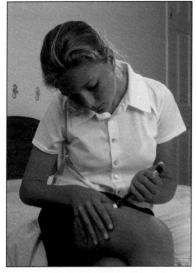

What other ways of using insulin are being researched?

TASKS

1 Think about your activities today and what you have eaten.
   Write down the times when:
   a insulin would be telling your liver to remove some glucose from your blood
   b your body would need to take some glucose back out of storage from the liver.

2 Draw a flow chart to show how insulin controls the level of glucose in your blood.

3 Plan a day's menu for a diabetic person.

4 Make a poster that explains homeostasis.

5 Find out what you can about Type 1 and Type 2 diabetes. What are the symptoms of diabetes?

6 **Forensic testing for glucose.**
   Portfolio Unit 1

The vast majority of **microorganisms** are harmless. However, some microorganisms cause disease when they get into your body.

Some human diseases are caused by bacteria. Boils are caused by the **bacterium** *Staphylococcus aureus*.

Some human diseases are caused by **viruses**. These include measles, rubella and mumps.

A person with measles develops a fever, and has a runny nose and a cough. Their eyelids become puffy. A blotchy red rash starts on the head and neck and spreads over the body.

Rubella, or German measles, is usually a mild disease for adults and children but very dangerous to unborn babies. When a person catches rubella, a rash appears on their face and spreads over their body and their limbs. The glands of their neck usually become swollen.

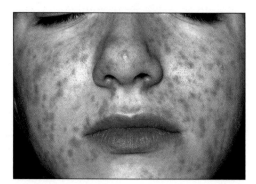

A child with rubella.

Mumps is a disease caused by a virus that infects the salivary glands and makes them swell. Some people who catch mumps don't show any symptoms, or they feel only slightly unwell.

When the polio virus infects someone, it can attack their nerves. If it does, it can paralyse the infected person.

a Make a list of human diseases caused by viruses.

b Find out which diseases caused by viruses can kill.

A few diseases of humans are caused by **fungi**. These include athlete's foot and ringworm, which are common, mild skin diseases.

c Very few diseases of humans are caused by fungi. Find out what organisms get the most serious fungal diseases.

How diseases spread

Diseases caused by microorganisms are spread in many different ways.

- Touch: athlete's foot is spread by touching a contaminated towel or changing room floor.
- Droplets in the air: when you sneeze or cough, you spray the air around with droplets of mucus. Measles, mumps and rubella are all spread in this way. And of course, this is how you usually catch cold (although these viruses are also spread by touch).

A sneeze!

- Dust: some microorganisms, such as tuberculosis (TB) and chickenpox, can be spread on dust in the air.

- Faeces: microorganisms such as the polio virus can be spread by faeces. Usually this is transferred by unwashed hands or carried by flies.

- Animals: mosquitoes carry the microorganism that causes malaria.

- Blood: HIV, the virus that causes AIDS, is spread by blood.

A mosquito taking blood and spreading malaria.

H **More on the spread of disease** CD-ROM

TASKS

1 Diseases can spread very rapidly. In the UK in 2001 foot and mouth, a disease of animals caused by a virus, infected cattle and sheep. The infected herds of cattle and sheep were slaughtered to try to stop the disease from spreading. Look at the graph, which shows the number of new infected cases identified every day.

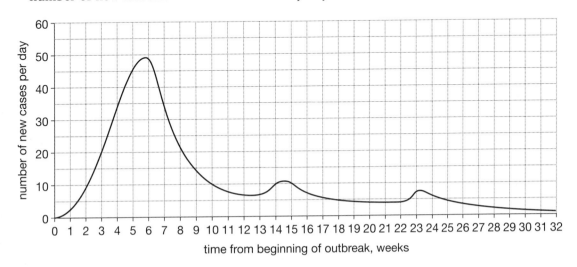

    a What type of organism causes foot and mouth disease?
    b When was the peak of the foot and mouth infection?
    c Try to find out what scientists think was the cause of the outbreak.
    d Try to find out how the disease was spread.

2.11 Keeping infection out!

If microbiologists know how a disease is spread, it may be possible to prevent it.

Stopping the spread of diseases

Ahlete's foot is a minor disease spread by touch. You can prevent it by avoiding contaminated surfaces or by keeping your feet cool and dry so that the fungus cannot grow.

For more serious diseases, infected people must be kept away from others.

To avoid diseases spread by droplets, you could stay away from crowded places, but in many cases this is not practical! It also helps to breathe through your nose. Your nose can filter out harmful microorganisms.

It's very difficult to prevent infections spread by dust. In situations where infection is possible, one method of prevention is to wear a protective mask.

To prevent infection from microorganisms in faeces, always wash your hands after going to the toilet. Flies should also be kept away from food.

For diseases carried by insects, use a spray to prevent bites. Sometimes it is possible to take preventive drugs. Some countries have managed to kill the insects that carry and spread the disease.

For diseases carried by blood, you must avoid contact with any blood that is contaminated.

Keep away from crowded places ...

a Give one example of a disease spread by droplet infection, one spread by touch and one spread by faeces. For each disease, what would you do to try to prevent it?

Examining a blood sample.

Studying microorganisms in the lab

Scientists studying diseases need to grow the microorganisms in the laboratory. They must:

- be careful not to get infected by the microorganisms
- make sure that microorganisms don't escape
- when studying one microorganism in particular, keep other microorganisms out.

To do this, scientists use a process called **aseptic technique**.

The glassware and other equipment is sterilised.

The scientist wears protective clothing. The microorganisms must stay in the lab!

The loop used to transfer microorganisms is sterilised in a Bunsen flame.

Microorganisms are transferred carefully onto the **agar plate**, keeping others out.

b How do microbiologists protect themselves against microorganisms?

c How is the transferring loop sterilised?

TASKS

1 Produce a health education leaflet or poster explaining how to avoid catching diseases.

2 Try to find out how surgical instruments are sterilised.

3 Why are disposable syringes used when taking blood samples?

4 People visiting a restaurant are struck down by a mystery illness. The owners think the water supply may have become contaminated.
How would you test the water to see if it contains bacteria?

5 **Using aseptic technique to test water for contamination by bacteria**
Portfolio Unit 1

2.12 Producing food safely

Disease is often spread by food. In the UK, 5.5 million people suffered from food poisoning at some time in 2001. Most of these cases were caused by food eaten outside the home.

You get food poisoning when the food you are eating has been contaminated with microorganisms.

Microorganisms get into food in several ways.

Microorganisms are found on the surface of foods.

How food is contaminated

Most bacteria on food are killed when the food is cooked properly. So a knife that has been used to cut raw meat should not then be used to cut cooked meat. This is because the bacteria on the raw meat will be transferred to the cooked meat. The bacteria breed quickly on the cooked meat because it is warm.

a Why should food be cooked properly?

b Why should the same knife not be used to cut raw meat and cooked meat?

Food can become contaminated in restaurants. In the restaurant kitchen, any dirty work surfaces will have many microorganisms on them. Food prepared on dirty work surfaces will pick up microorganisms. People who work in the kitchen must also make sure their hands are kept clean while preparing food. Their hair should be covered so that it does not contaminate the food.

c Write down two ways in which food poisoning could be spread in a restaurant.

We can, however, prevent contamination of food by microorganisms.

Preventing food contamination

Disinfectants are chemicals that kill microorganisms. They do this very effectively and are therefore usually harmful or irritant chemicals. Disinfectants are used to clean work surfaces and sinks.

Antiseptics are also chemicals that kill microorganisms, but they are safe to use on human skin. People who work with food should use antiseptic wipes on their hands after washing them.

Sterilisation is often used to kill microorganisms in food itself. This is usually done by heating the food to a high temperature. Food packaged in cans is always sterilised.

d What is sterilisation?

Stewart works on the production line at a factory producing cakes and biscuits. All of the staff have to be very aware of hygiene.

Stewart follows a strict hygiene code. He is wearing a clean white coat and a hat to cover his hair.

e Suggest something he has to do before he starts work and then regularly during the day.

Every effort is made to ensure that the food leaving the factory is not contaminated with microorganisms.

Unfortunately it is poor hygiene in places like restaurants, hotels and hospitals that causes food poisoning.

Stewart working on the production line.

TASKS

1 a What is a disinfectant?
   b What is an antiseptic?
   c What are antiseptics and disinfectants usually used for?

2 Producing food that is safe and free from dangerous bacteria is very important.
   Joe is setting up a business that will produce sliced processed meat products for supermarkets. His staff will have to handle the meat.
   Plan a leaflet for Joe, giving clear hygiene advice to his employees.

3 **Investigating the effect of disinfectants on the growth of bacteria**
   Portfolio Unit 1, Unit 3

When you get a sore throat, it normally lasts for about a week. You recover because of your immune system.

Gita's throat feels sore. Bacteria have invaded the cells lining her throat. Her immune system swings into action and produces chemicals called **antibodies**.

Gita recovers, but her body remembers the infection. Antibodies can now be produced very quickly and are ready to defend her body if the same bacterium tries to invade it.

Immunisation

When you entered secondary school, you were probably given an injection of the BCG **vaccine**. This is to make you immune to TB (tuberculosis). It is called an **immunisation**.

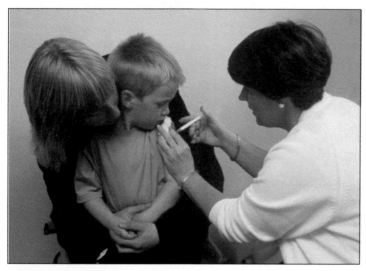

A BCG vaccination.

The polio vaccine is often given on a lump of sugar.

Many vaccines are made using dead microorganisms. Others are made using microorganisms that are so weak that they can no longer cause disease. When these are put into your blood, your body produces antibodies against them. The microorganisms are destroyed, and you are now ready to fight these microorganisms if you ever become infected. You are now immunised against the disease.

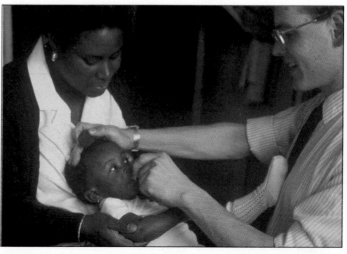

A polio 'vaccination'.

a What do vaccines contain?

A weak bacterium from the vaccine in the bloodstream.

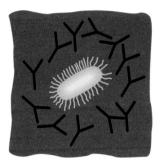
The body produces antibodies.

The bacteria are killed. Antibodies are produced very quickly if you get a real infection.

As well as protecting people, vaccines get rid of disease. Polio paralysed or killed many people in the 1950s. Now the disease has been wiped out in the UK.

Most young children receive an immunisation against MMR (measles, mumps and rubella together). We also hope to get rid of these diseases. Given together, it is easier to make sure that everyone is immunised against all three. It is also better to get the injections over with in one go!

b What else do vaccines do, besides *preventing* infection?

Sometimes your body needs help to defend itself against invading microorganisms because:

• your body cannot produce antibodies quickly enough
• the microorganism defends itself against your immune system.

That's when you need antibiotics or antiviral drugs.

More on the MMR vaccine

TASKS

1 a How do vaccines immunise you against a disease?
  b In what ways can you receive a vaccine?

2 Measles, German measles (rubella) and mumps are usually fairly mild diseases caused by viruses. Complications can, however, develop, and these can cause serious damage. From October 1988, a vaccine was used to immunise children against these diseases.

The table shows the number of cases of measles every two years from 1989 up to 1999.

What effect did the vaccine have on the number of cases of measles?

School year ending	Measles cases
1989	26 000
1991	9 700
1993	9 600
1995	7 500
1997	4 000
1999	2 400

Smoking

We all know that smoking cigarettes can be harmful. Certainly a smoker can be expected to live, on average, a shorter life than a non-smoker.

Tobacco smoke contains over 4000 chemicals. These chemicals are either gases or tiny particles. Some of these chemicals are carcinogens (chemicals causing cancer).

a What health problems do smokers suffer from?

The photograph shows a section of a lung from a smoker. Look at the damage that smoking has done.

But smokers are not the only ones to suffer the effects of cigarette smoke. People who work in places where smoking takes place can suffer from other people smoking. People who inhale the smoke from nearby smokers are said to be engaged in passive smoking.

b List some workers that might be at risk from passive smoking.

The immediate effects to passive smokers may include sore throat, cough, sore eyes and headaches. The long-term effects to passive smokers are an increased risk of heart disease and lung cancer.

Jenny is an Environmental Health Officer. Part of her job is to explain to people the risks of passive smoking.

c Why has it been difficult to prove that passive smoking causes lung cancer?

Nicotine in tobacco is a very dangerous drug. Drugs can affect health.

Drugs can be divided into two groups, medical and recreational.

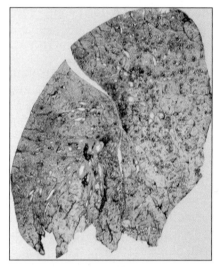

This lung has been damaged by deposits of tar from cigarette smoke.

Medical drugs

Most people take medicines at some time. It is important that all medicines are taken according to the instructions. If people take too many medical drugs they could damage their liver.

Sometimes doctors need to prescribe drugs that are addictive and dangerous. Patients who are terminally ill and in great pain may be given drugs such as morphine. This relieves pain effectively. Doctors are very careful to prescribe the correct amount to make sure the drug does not cause any problems.

Occasionally doctors prescribe cannabis as a medical drug. Cannabis helps to relieve the symptoms of a disease of the nervous system called multiple sclerosis.

Recreational drugs

Recreational drugs are drugs taken by people for pleasure. They include caffeine, nicotine and alcohol. Some of these are dangerous to health: too much alcohol destroys liver cells, and eventually the liver stops working; smoking increases the risk of heart disease and cancer.

It is legal for adults to buy cigarettes and alcohol.

Other recreational drugs are illegal. There are many different illegal drugs, including cannabis, ecstasy, cocaine and heroin. These drugs are illegal because they are very addictive and harmful to your body. Other chemicals, such as solvents, can also affect people's physical and mental health.

d Which drug is used both as a medical and as a recreational drug?

When people become addicted to drugs their body cannot work without the drug. They suffer from withdrawal symptoms if they fail to take the drug.

e Many people who are smokers want to give up smoking. Nicotine patches can help them give up smoking. How do these help?

TASKS

1 Why is important that pregnant women not smoke cigarettes or drink alcohol?

2 Why is it difficult to give up smoking or drinking alcohol?

3 What are the dangers of passive smoking?

4 Mina says that all drugs should be banned. Explain why this is not a good idea.

5 Forensic testing for alcohol
Portfolio Unit 1   CD-ROM

You can catch some diseases from other people. Such diseases are called **contagious**. Diseases like flu, measles and mumps are contagious.

Some diseases are not caught but are inherited from your parents.

a Describe what is meant by the word inherited.

Parents pass on characteristics to their children in their genes. Sometimes these genes carry the information for a disease. The information sometimes causes the child to be affected by the disease. Such inherited diseases are called **genetic diseases**, and are rare.

Cystic fibrosis and Huntington's chorea are genetic diseases.

Cystic fibrosis affects about 1 in 2000 children. People can carry the gene for cystic fibrosis but not suffer from the disease themselves. These people are called **carriers**. If both parents carry the gene for cystic fibrosis, there is a risk that their children may be born with the disease. The parents may not know that they carry the gene for cystic fibrosis.

b What other characteristics are inherited from parents?

Cystic fibrosis is a disease that affects the digestive system and the breathing system. The digestive system and the breathing system usually contain a sticky solution called mucus. People with cystic fibrosis develop mucus that is thicker and stickier than normal.

This mucus blocks the airways in the breathing system and the tubes in the digestive system. This causes the patient to have difficulty in breathing and absorbing food. The blocked airways can easily become infected. These infections can cause damage to the lungs. This makes breathing even more difficult.

People with cystic fibrosis need vigorous physiotherapy to dislodge the blocked mucus. They need to attend physiotherapy every few days.

At the moment, there is no cure for cystic fibrosis.

Huntington's chorea is a disease that affects the nervous system. It stops cells in the brain from working properly. People who develop the disease move in a jerky, abnormal way, and lose their mental abilities.

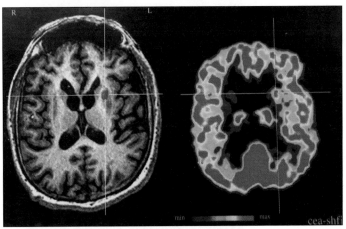

In patients with Huntington's chorea, the outer layer of the brain gets smaller. Spaces in the brain called ventricles enlarge.

The disease does not usually appear in patients until the age of 35–40. It gets worse over the next 15 to 20 years. Like cystic fibrosis, it is a rare disease. It affects about 1 in 18 000 people. But unlike cystic fibrosis, people can't be carriers only. If a person has the gene for Huntington's chorea, that person will develop the disease.

H More on genetic diseases CD-ROM

TASKS

1 Which two organ systems does cystic fibrosis affect in people?

2 Explain why the diseases cystic fibrosis and Huntington's chorea are different from diseases like influenza.

3 Some people are carriers for cystic fibrosis.
a Explain what is meant by the expression 'a carrier for cystic fibrosis'.
b Explain why a person cannot be a carrier for Huntington's chorea.

4 Explain why cystic fibrosis is rare.

Case Study: Sports science biomechanics analyst

Mark works for a company that analyses how athletes move during their sporting activities.

The equipment Mark uses can detect movement in muscles. The movement is caused by signals from the brain. These signals are called nerve impulses. Nerve cells are specially adapted to carry impulses rapidly around the body.

Mark also monitors how each athlete positions their feet on the ground as they run. Mark uses this information to help athletes run faster and more efficiently.

Mark can also use equipment to measure breathing rate. Our breathing rate increases as we exercise. When we exercise our muscle cells need more energy. To provide the extra energy our muscle cells need to carry out aerobic respiration at a faster rate. Oxygen is needed for respiration. To provide this extra oxygen our breathing rate increases.

During hard exercise people can't take in enough oxygen to meet the energy demands of the muscle cells. When this happens anaerobic respiration starts to take place in our muscle cells. Athletes need to be aware of anaerobic respiration because it is very inefficient. During anaerobic respiration less energy is released, causing the athlete to slow down. Anaerobic respiration also produces lactic acid. A build up of lactic acid in our cells causes pain in the muscles. Athletes that can avoid anaerobic respiration will be able to continue at a greater speed.

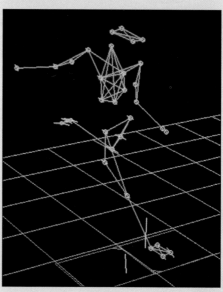

Computer display of a wire frame footballer about to kick a ball.

1 Explain why it is important for nerve impulses to travel rapidly around the body.

2 When we exercise harder our breathing rate increases. Explain why.

3 During aerobic respiration our cells use glucose and oxygen to provide energy. Carbon dioxide and water are produced during the reaction. Write the word equation for aerobic respiration.

4 Explain why an athlete will slow down if anaerobic respiration is taking place in their muscle cells.

1 When you eat a meal the food passes through the different organs of your digestive system. This list shows the organs that make up your digestive system. They are in the wrong order.

  a Copy out the list in the correct order.

      1 large intestine

      2 mouth

      3 small intestine

      4 gullet (oesophagus)

      5 stomach   [4]

  b Describe what happens to the food when it is in the small intestine.   [2]

2 The human heart has four chambers.

  left atrium   **left ventricle**   **right atrium**   **right ventricle**

  Write down the name of the chamber that:

  a receives blood from the lungs   [1]

  b pumps the blood out of the heart and all around the body   [1]

  c pumps the blood to the lungs   [1]

  d receives blood from the body.   [1]

3 As you breathe in, air travels down to your lungs. The list shows the different parts of the breathing system. They are in the wrong order. Copy out the list in the correct order.

      1 bronchus

      2 alveoli

      3 trachea

      4 bronchioles   [3]

  b Which gas moves from the lungs into the blood?   [1]

  c Which gas moves from the blood into the lungs?   [1]

  d Describe what happens to the gas after it has moved from the blood into the lungs.   [2]

4   **a** List the names of **three** groups of microorganisms.   [3]

  b Give **three** examples of diseases caused by microorganisms.   [3]

  c Give **two** examples of useful microorganisms.   [2]

5 A small number of microorganisms cause disease.

  a Give **two** examples of diseases caused by bacteria.   [2]

  b What type of drug is used to treat infections caused by bacteria?   [1]

  c What type of organism causes athlete's foot?   [1]

  d Give **three** ways in which microorganisms are spread.   [3]

6 Anna works in a food processing factory. She must make sure all the cans of food produced are free from microorganisms. How does she make sure that:

  a work surfaces are free from microorganisms?   [1]

  b her hands are free from microorganisms?   [2]

  c The food leaving the factory in cans is free from microorganisms?   [1]

7 Gita is off school recovering from a sore throat.

    a What groups of microorganisms cause disease? [3]

    b What chemicals did Gita produce to help her fight off the disease? [1]

8   **a** How do doctors immunise you against a disease? [1]

    b Name **three** vaccinations given to children in this country. [3]

9 Tara wants to increase the number of red blood cells in her body before the race.

    a What is the job of the red blood cells? [1]

    b Explain why it would be an advantage for Tara to have more red blood cells inside her body. [3]

    c As Tara is running she is breathing out more carbon dioxide. Describe how carbon dioxide moves from the blood into the lungs. [3]

10 **a** As Tara runs, she becomes very warm. Describe **two** things Tara's body will do to help keep her cool. [4]

    b At the end of the race Tara becomes cold and starts to shiver. Describe **two** other things Tara's body will do to help keep her warm. [4]

    c Someone from St John's Ambulance has arrived to take care of Tara. Describe what this person will do to help keep Tara warm. [3]

11 As Tara eats chocolate her body tries to control the amount of sugar in her blood.

    a Which of these hormones controls the amount of sugar in Tara's blood?
    adrenaline   insulin   oestrogen [1]

    b Write down the meaning of the scientific term **hormone**. [2]

    c Which of the following organs produces the hormone that controls Tara's blood sugar levels?
    heart   liver   pancreas [1]

    d Which of the following organs takes the sugar from Tara's blood and stores it?
    heart   liver   pancreas [1]

    e Homeostasis is the name given to the process that tries to keep all things constant inside our bodies.
List two other things, apart from blood sugar, controlled by homeostasis. [2]

12 Microorganisms can be spread in several ways. Use the following words to explain how each disease is spread:

touch   droplets   dust   faeces
animals   blood

    a Measles, mumps and rubella [1]

    b Athlete's foot [1]

    c AIDS [1]

    d Polio [1]

    e TB [1]

    f Malaria [1]

13 Anthony works in the food industry. Explain how he

    a uses chemicals to kill microorganisms [2]

    b prevents bacteria from his body getting into the food [2]

    c kills microorganisms in the food. [1]

14 Dean had a BCG vaccination against TB.

    a What do vaccines contain? [2]

    b How do vaccines help to protect Dean against future TB infection? [2]

    c What is this process of protection against disease called? [1]

15 Research has been carried out in Scotland on the effect of smoking on deaths from lung cancer. Some of the results are shown below.

Number of cigarettes per day	Number of deaths from lung cancer in one year	
	Men	Women
0	82	204
1–14	260	422
15–24	1005	852
Over 25	693	133
Ex-smokers	260	89

a Find the number of people that have died from lung cancer and that
 i never smoked [1]
 ii did smoke. [1]

b In which group of smokers was the risk of dying from lung cancer highest? [1]

c What effect does giving up cigarettes have on the chances of dying from lung cancer? [2]

The same researchers also investigated the effect of passive smoking on the deaths from lung cancer in people who do not smoke. The data are shown in the table below.

	Number of deaths from lung cancer in one year	
Exposure to tobacco smoke	Men	Women
No	23	43
Yes	59	161

e Find the total number of people who died from lung cancer who:
 i did not take in smoke [1]
 ii smoked passively. [1]

f What do the results suggest about passive smoking and lung cancer? [1]

g Explain why scientists cannot be absolutely certain of this conclusion. [2]

16 The diagram shows the structure of Tara's respiratory system.

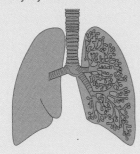

a Label the positions of the bronchi, bronchioles and alveoli. [3]

b When blood returning from Tara's muscles reaches her heart, explain why:

 i the oxygen concentration is low [1]
 ii the carbon dioxide concentration is high. [1]

c Tara's heart pumps blood to her lungs to pick up oxygen. Explain why:
 i there are bicuspid and tricuspid valves between the atria and ventricles of the heart [1]
 ii the wall of the left ventricle is four times thicker than the right ventricle. [1]

d Complete the table below.

	The air that Tara breathes in	The air that Tara breathes out
Oxygen concentration %		
Carbon dioxide concentration %		

[4]

e As Tara runs the race, the oxygen reaching her muscles may be in short supply. Explain the process that enables her to keep running. [2]

f Write a word equation for the process in part **e**. [2]

17 Some diseases in humans are caused by the bacterium *Staphylococcus aureus*.

a Name one skin disease caused by *Staphylococcus aureus*.

b If this bacterium enters the body, it can cause serious diseases. The skin is normally an effective barrier to the bacterium entering the body. How is the bacterium kept out if the skin becomes broken or cut? [2]

c Infections caused by *Staphylococcus aureus* normally require antibiotics to cure them. When a new antibiotic is discovered, what must scientists do before it can be used to cure disease in patients? [2]

Obtaining useful chemicals

Case study: Testing for illegal substances

Terri works part-time in a supermarket. One day a man from the local Public Analyst's laboratory came to the supermarket and took away some bottles of orange squash. He told Terri that the squash would be tested to see if it contained illegal food colourings.

Many foods contain artificial colourings. The colours make the foods more attractive to shoppers. Only certain approved colourings are allowed to be added to foods. It is illegal to add colourings that have not been approved.

At the Public Analyst's laboratory a sample of the orange squash is analysed using the technique of *paper chromatography* to identify the colouring in the squash.

A pencil line is drawn on a piece of chromatography paper. On this line a spot of the orange squash is placed, together with a spot of each of the colourings that might be in the squash. The chromatography paper is placed in a container called a chromatography tank, so that the end of the paper dips into a solvent. The container is covered with a lid and left for the solvent to rise up the paper.

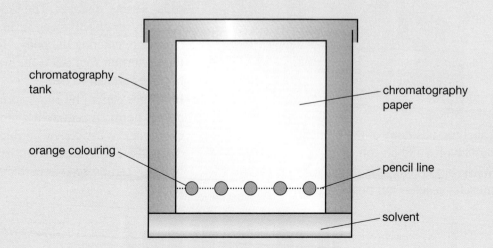

chromatography tank

chromatography paper

orange colouring

pencil line

solvent

After a few minutes the solvent has risen almost to the top of the paper. It carries the colourings with it. Different colourings are carried at different speeds. Each colouring reaches a different level on the paper.

Colouring 1 is from the orange squash. Colourings 2, 3 and 4 are permitted food colourings. Colouring 5 is an illegal food colouring.

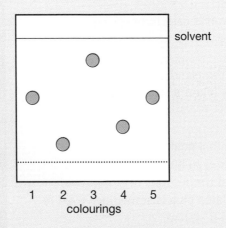

1 Suggest why some colourings are not allowed in foods.

2 Why is a lid placed on the chromatography tank?

3 Does the orange squash from the supermarket contain an illegal colouring? Explain your answer.

4 What do you think the Public Analyst will do about this squash?

How this chapter can help you with your portfolio

Unit I and Unit 3

What you learn in this chapter will help you with these portfolio tasks:

- Preparation of barium sulfate
- Preparation of ammonium sulfate
- Concentration effects
- Indigestion tablets
- Forensic analysis
- Preparation of silver chloride
- Smaller is quicker
- Water pollution

Unit I

This chapter may also help you with this case study on your CD-ROM:

- Cement works

Using gold

The jewellery worn by this model is made from the metal gold. Gold is used to make jewellery because it does not go dull and rust. This is because gold does not react with air like most metals do.

Gold is also a soft metal, so it is easy to make into the shapes needed for jewellery.

a Gold jewellery that is thousands of years old still looks as good today as when it was made. Suggest why.

In Chapter 4 you will learn that gold is a very good conductor of electricity. It is even better than copper. Gold is used for making electrical connections in computers and hi-fi systems. A gold-plated plug is sometimes used to connect headphones to a hi-fi system.

b Why is gold not used for electrical wiring?

c Gold is used as money. Many coins have been made from gold. Suggest why.

Gold is an **element**. This means that it is made from particles that are gold atoms. No other substance is present.

What metal would you want to use for caps or fillings? Find out whether this is a safe choice.

Where does gold come from?

Most metals are found combined in the Earth with other elements. Because gold does not react easily with other elements, it is found just as gold.

Gold can be found as small fragments in fast flowing rivers.

These people are panning for gold.

Using sulfur

Sulfur is another element. It is a brittle, yellow solid and a non-metal.

Sulfur reacts with many metals to form **compounds** called sulfides.

The most important use of sulfur is in the manufacture of sulfuric acid. Fertilisers, explosives, pigments, detergents, soaps, dyes and plastics are all made using sulfuric acid.

Sulfur is used to harden rubber. This is an essential process in the making of car tyres. It is called **vulcanising**.

Sulfur is also one of the chemicals in gunpowder.

d An eraser used to rub out pencil marks is made of rubber. This rubber has not been vulcanised with sulfur. Why not?

Where does sulfur come from?

Crystals of sulfur can be seen around hot springs.

e What does this photograph tell you about the solubility of sulfur in water?

In some parts of the world large deposits of sulfur are found underground. Instead of digging a mine to get this sulfur, hot water is used to melt the sulfur and force it to the surface.

TASKS

1 On the student CD-ROM you will find a database giving the information you need to know about 20 elements. Use the database to find the names and symbols of these 20 elements. Divide these elements into two lists:
a metals and non-metals
b solids, liquids and gases at room temperature (20°C).
Portfolio Unit 3 d2

3.2 Atoms, compounds and formulae

Atoms

All materials are made of **atoms**. Each atom is made up of three different types of particle: **protons**, **neutrons** and **electrons**. Electrons are much smaller and weigh far less than protons or neutrons.

In the centre of each atom is a very tiny core, called the **nucleus**. The nucleus is made up of tightly packed protons and neutrons.

Electrons move rapidly round the nucleus.

a What are the names of the three particles that make up all atoms?

b Where is most of the mass in an atom?

Each element has its own type of atom, made up of different numbers of protons, neutrons and electrons. All atoms of the same element have the same number of protons and electrons. The diagram shows this arrangement for a sodium atom.

Each element has its own **symbol**. Scientists around the world use these symbols. On page 211 of this book you will find a list of the symbols you need to learn.

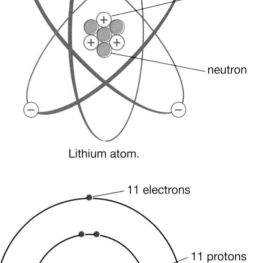

Lithium atom.

11 electrons

11 protons

12 neutrons

Compounds and formulae

Atoms from different elements combine to form **compounds**. You can tell what is in a compound by looking at its **formula**.

Sodium and chlorine atoms join together to form the compound sodium chloride. The symbol for sodium is Na. The symbol for chlorine is Cl. Sodium chloride has the formula NaCl.

c What elements are combined in calcium carbonate?

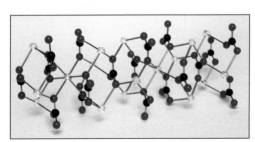

This ball and stick model represents calcium carbonate.

$CaCO_3$

A bottle containing calcium carbonate. The formula is a shorthand way of showing what is in the compound.

Often different numbers of atoms join together to form a compound. The number of each atom in a compound is shown by the formula of the compound.

Methane has the formula CH_4. This means that each carbon atom is joined to four hydrogen atoms.

d How many atoms are in the formula of copper sulfate, $CuSO_4$?

e How many different elements does copper sulfate contain?

Many of the materials we use are **mixtures**. A mixture may contain just elements, it may be made up of compounds only, or it could contain both elements and compounds. The components of a mixture are not chemically combined. Air is a mixture of elements such as oxygen, nitrogen and argon, and compounds such as carbon dioxide.

Formulae of elements

Chlorine is an element. In nature it exists as two chlorine atoms joined together. The symbol for this is Cl_2.

Iron is an element, but it exists as a single atom, Fe.

f Here are the formulae of some elements, as they exist in nature. Write down their names.

Al Br_2 Ca H_2 N_2 Zn

 **More on atomic structure**

TASKS

1 The CD-ROM contains a database of information about elements and compounds. Use this database to find the formula, number of atoms in each formula and the state (solid, liquid or gas) at room temperature of each of the following substances:

aluminium   ammonia   barium sulfate   copper carbonate
fluorine   oxygen   potassium   sulfuric acid

Portfolio Unit 1 e2

2 Using the information on the CD-ROM, divide the substances in this list into two columns, 'elements' and 'compounds'.

aluminium   barium chloride   calcium oxide   carbon   lead   methane
silver   sodium hydroxide   sulfur   hydrogen oxide (water)   zinc

Portfolio Unit 1 e2

Limestone

Limestone is a **mineral** that is mined from quarries. The rock is blasted with explosives.

a What problems might you experience if you lived near a limestone quarry?

Limestone has many uses. Since it is found quite pure, for some jobs it can be used straight from the ground. It can also be used to make other useful materials. When limestone is heated with sodium carbonate and sand it makes glass.

Limestone is also used to make cement, which is used to make concrete. Many modern buildings are made using concrete.

Farmers use limestone to cure excess acidity in soils. Quicklime, which is made from limestone, can also be used to neutralise acidity in soils or in water supplies.

The Sydney Opera House is made of concrete.

b Why is very acidic soil a problem?

Limestone is made from calcium carbonate, $CaCO_3$.

Marble

Marble is also a rock that is made from calcium carbonate. Limestone is turned into marble under high pressure and temperature deep in the Earth's crust.

Marble is much harder and stronger than limestone, and has a very attractive appearance. Since marble is almost pure calcium carbonate, it can be used straight from the ground.

c Suggest why marble is used for public buildings.

Testing for calcium

Both limestone and marble contain the metal calcium. A simple **flame test** proves this.

A little of the rock powder is added to hydrochloric acid. A flame test wire, which is a piece of wire made from an unreactive metal, is then dipped into the solution. When the wire is placed in a very hot Bunsen burner flame (a blue flame), a red colour appears. This shows that the compound contains calcium. Other metals give other colours to the flame.

 **More on testing for metals** CD-ROM

What element might this metal contain?

TASKS

1 Some compounds contain a metal. We can use flame tests to find out which metal a compound contains. The table shows the colour of a Bunsen burner flame when a compound containing each of the metals is tested.

   Five compounds are tested using a flame. Finish this table showing the results of these tests. All the compounds are chlorides.

Element	Symbol	Flame colour
calcium	Ca	red
copper	Cu	green
iron	Fe	yellow sparks
lead	Pb	blue
potassium	K	lilac
sodium	Na	yellow

Compound	Name of compound	Formula of compound	Colour of flame test
A	potassium chloride		lilac
B			red
C	iron chloride		
D			green
E	sodium chloride		

Portfolio Unit 1 c2, 3 d2

2 **Forensic analysis**
   Portfolio Unit 1, Unit 3 CD-ROM

3 **Water pollution**
   Portfolio Unit 1, Unit 3 CD-ROM

4 **Cement works**
   Portfolio Unit 1, Unit 3 CD-ROM

3.4 Writing equations

Chemical equations

A chemical **equation** is a shorthand way of writing down what happens in a chemical reaction.

- The substances that are reacting with each other, the **reactants**, are written on the left of the equation.
- The substances made in the reaction, the **products**, are written on the right of the equation.
- An arrow shows the direction of the reaction:

    reactants → products

The simplest equations to write are word equations. The names of reactants and products are written in the equation.

A symbol equation gives more information. The formulae of the reactants and products are used.

Quicklime

When limestone is heated strongly, it breaks up to form quicklime. Quicklime is calcium oxide. This is an example of thermal **decomposition**.

A word equation for this reaction shows calcium carbonate, the chemical name for limestone, on the left. On the right are the products – calcium oxide and carbon dioxide.

    calcium carbonate (limestone) → calcium oxide (quicklime) + carbon dioxide

The symbol equation for this reaction contains the formulae of calcium carbonate, calcium oxide and carbon dioxide.

$$CaCO_3 \rightarrow CaO + CO_2$$

a What does the formula tell you about each compound?

b Suggest why a symbol equation could be more useful than a word equation.

 **More on chemical equations** CD-ROM

Testing for carbonate

Carbon dioxide gas is given off when calcium carbonate, or any other carbonate, reacts with an acid such as hydrochloric acid. This reaction can be used to test for the presence of carbonate in a compound.

A little of the powdered substance is added to hydrochloric acid in a test tube. The gas produced is bubbled through limewater.

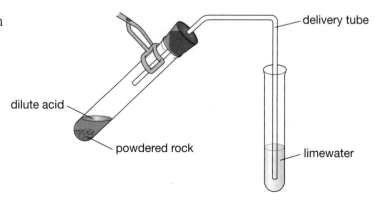

dilute acid

powdered rock

delivery tube

limewater

If a carbonate is present, carbon dioxide is given off. This turns the limewater from clear and colourless to a cloudy white.

c Why do you think powdered rock is used for this test instead of a lump of rock?

This is a word equation for the reaction between calcium carbonate and hydrochloric acid.

calcium carbonate + hydrochloric acid → calcium chloride + water + carbon dioxide

The first step in writing a symbol equation is to put the formula of each substance underneath the name.

calcium carbonate + hydrochloric acid → calcium chloride + water + carbon dioxide
$$CaCO_3 \quad + \quad HCl \quad \rightarrow \quad CaCl_2 \quad + H_2O + \quad CO_2$$

If we add up the number of symbols, and therefore the number of atoms, of each element on each side of the equation, the numbers do not match.

$$1 \times Ca, \ 1 \times C, \ 3 \times O, \ 1 \times H, \ 1 \times Cl \rightarrow 1 \times Ca, \ 2 \times Cl, \ 2 \times H, \ 1 \times O, \ 1 \times C, \ 2 \times O$$

To make these numbers equal on each side, the equation must be balanced. This can be done by adding the number 2 in front of the HCl.

$$CaCO_3 + 2HCl \rightarrow CaCl_2 + H_2O + CO_2$$

This means that we have two lots of HCl on the left, so the numbers of symbols are now equal.

$$1 \times Ca, \ 1 \times C, \ 3 \times O, \ 2 \times H, \ 2 \times Cl \rightarrow 1 \times Ca, \ 2 \times Cl, \ 2 \times H, \ 1 \times O, \ 1 \times C, \ 2 \times O$$

d Why is it important to balance a symbol equation?

TASKS

1 These word equations have had the formulae written beneath them, but the symbol equations have not been balanced. Complete the symbol equations by balancing them.

a sodium + chlorine → sodium chloride
$$Na \quad + \quad Cl_2 \quad \rightarrow \quad NaCl$$
b magnesium + hydrochloric acid → magnesium chloride + hydrogen
$$Mg \quad + \quad HCl \quad \rightarrow \quad MgCl_2 \quad + \quad H_2$$
c copper oxide + hydrochloric acid → copper chloride + water
$$CuO \quad + \quad HCl \quad \rightarrow \quad CuCl_2 \quad + \quad H_2O$$
d aluminium + oxygen → aluminium oxide
$$Al \quad + \quad O_2 \quad \rightarrow \quad Al_2O_3$$

 **More questions** CD-ROM

103

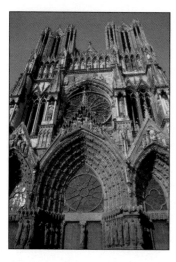

These photographs are of a cathedral built from limestone.

Over many years the limestone has **corroded** so that you cannot see much of the original detail. It has been corroded by acids in rain.

Should historical sculptures be restored? If so, with what materials?

a Why has the corrosion of limestone increased over the past century?

Acid rain

Limestone is made from calcium carbonate. The equation shows the reaction of calcium carbonate with sulfuric acid.

calcium carbonate + sulfuric acid → calcium sulfate + carbon dioxide + water
$$CaCO_3 \quad + \quad H_2SO_4 \quad \rightarrow \quad CaSO_4 \quad + \quad CO_2 \quad + H_2O$$

The concentration of acids in rainwater is very low. This makes the reaction slow. It takes many years for limestone statues to be badly corroded.

If a piece of limestone is added to a more concentrated solution of acid, the reaction is quicker. The photograph shows pieces of limestone in different concentrations of acid. The reaction gives off bubbles of carbon dioxide.

b How do the photographs show that the more concentrated acid is reacting more quickly?

Changing the speed of reaction

The more concentrated a solution, the quicker the reaction. But there are other things that can make a reaction go faster or slower.

As temperature increases, the speed of the reaction also increases.

c If you turn an oven up to a higher temperature the food inside cooks more quickly. Why?

The photograph shows different-sized pieces of limestone added to dilute hydrochloric acid. This shows that smaller pieces react more quickly than larger pieces.

On the left is a lump of limestone and on the right is limestone powder.

d A whole potato placed in boiling water cooks slowly. But if the potato is cut into pieces first it cooks quickly. Why?

A **catalyst** is a substance that speeds up a reaction but is unchanged at the end of the reaction. The photograph shows the catalyst manganese(IV) oxide being added to hydrogen peroxide.

Before the catalyst is added a reaction takes place, but it is very slow. You can hardly notice it happening. As the catalyst is added, the reaction speeds up, giving off oxygen gas.

e 0.2 g of manganese(IV) oxide is added to some hydrogen peroxide solution. When the reaction has stopped, 0.2 g of manganese(IV) oxide remains. Explain why.

Hydrogen peroxide before and after adding manganese (IV) oxide.

 More on rate of reaction CD-ROM

TASKS

1 There are four things that change the speed of a reaction. Find them and write them down.

2 For each reaction described below, say whether it is fast or slow, and explain why.
   a An iron gate rusting.
   b Clothes being washed in a washing machine when only a small amount of washing powder has been added.
   c A large log burning on a fire.
   d Sliced vegetables being stir-fried in a wok.
   e Hydrogen peroxide solution left standing in a bottle.
   Portfolio Unit 3 b1, b2

3 **Smaller is quicker**
   Portfolio Unit 1, Unit 3 CD-ROM

4 **Concentration effects**
   Portfolio Unit 1, Unit 3 CD-ROM

 **More questions** CD-ROM

3.6 Crude oil

Crude oil is a thick, black, smelly liquid. Large quantities are transported by sea in tankers. As this photograph shows, when crude oil is spilled into the sea it causes enormous pollution problems.

a How might crude oil get spilled into the sea?

Crude oil is formed from the remains of dead animals and plants. The remains are compressed at high pressures and temperatures, deep within the Earth's crust. This takes millions of years.

Find out how oil spills are cleared up.

Crude oil is a mixture of chemicals called **hydrocarbons**. These substances are compounds made up of only the two elements hydrogen and carbon. Although the mixture has little use, when the compounds in the mixture are separated they are very useful.

Extracting the useful compounds

Fractional distillation is used to separate the crude oil into small groups of hydrocarbons, called **fractions**.

Crude oil is heated and turned into vapour in the fractionating column. Hydrocarbons with different boiling points condense as they pass up the column and are cooled. Fractions containing mixtures of hydrocarbons with similar boiling points are collected at different heights on the column. Fractions with high boiling points exit at the bottom of the column.

The fraction with the highest boiling point is bitumen. This is used for making roads.

b Which fraction has hydrocarbons with the lowest boiling points?

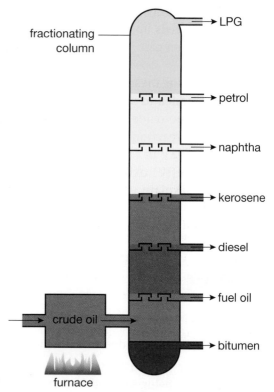

Most of the fractions are used as fuels, for example:

* gasoline, also called petrol, used for cars
* kerosene, also called paraffin, used for central heating and jet aircraft
* diesel, used for lorries
* liquefied petroleum gases, known as LPG (the hydrocarbons propane and butane), used as a fuel for central heating, camping and some cars.

The fractions used as fuels are **flammable**. This means they burn very easily.

The naphtha fraction from crude oil is used as a 'chemical feedstock'. The chemicals in this fraction are used to make a wide variety of materials, including plastics, medicines, textiles, paints and dyes.

Of the fractions separated from crude oil, far more petrol is used than any other. So much petrol is needed that some of the naphtha fraction is used to make more petrol. These two uses for the naphtha fraction compete with each other.

c What problems will this cause in the future as our supply of crude oil runs out?

These diagrams show the formulae of four of the hydrocarbons in crude oil. They are examples of **organic** compounds.

Organic compounds are made mainly of carbon. They usually contain hydrogen as well, and sometimes they include other elements such as oxygen or nitrogen. At one time scientists thought that organic compounds could only be made by living things, but nowadays many organic compounds can be made in the laboratory.

Inorganic compounds are *not* made mainly from carbon. Examples of inorganic compounds are sodium chloride ($NaCl$), copper(II) sulfate ($CuSO_4$) and nitric acid (HNO_3).

d What is the main difference between an organic compound and an inorganic compound?

More on fractional distillation

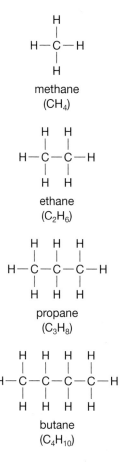

methane
(CH_4)

ethane
(C_2H_6)

propane
(C_3H_8)

butane
(C_4H_{10})

TASKS

1 The names and formulae of a number of compounds are shown below. Write down the number of atoms of each element in the compounds. Use this information to help you divide the compounds into two lists: organic compounds and inorganic compounds.

carbon dioxide, CO_2

ethane, C_2H_6

ethanoic acid, $C_2H_5CO_2H$

ethanol, C_2H_5OH

glucose, $C_6H_{12}O_6$

lead oxide, PbO

potassium nitrate, KNO_3

sulfuric acid, H_2SO_4

More questions

3.7 Salt

Separating salt

Salt is a very useful chemical. We use salt to improve the flavour of food. It is also scattered on icy roads to prevent cars from skidding.

The chemical name for salt is sodium chloride. Its formula is NaCl.

Salt is found deep within the Earth's crust mixed with sand and other impurities. The mixture is called **rock salt**. Rock salt is mined and crushed into a coarse powder for use on roads.

a The sodium chloride in rock salt melts the ice. What else in rock salt helps car tyres to grip the road?

We would not want to put rock salt on our food – the sodium chloride needs to be separated from the impurities. There are three simple steps to get pure salt:

- stir the rock salt in warm water until the sodium chloride has dissolved
- filter the mixture so that all the impurities are removed and only salt water is left
- heat the salt water until all the water has evaporated and only salt is left.

Rock salt.

Pure salt.

b Why does dissolving the sodium chloride help to separate it from impurities in the rock salt?

Solution mining of salt uses the same ideas. Water is pumped into the salt deposits under the ground. Because the sodium chloride dissolves in the water, sodium chloride solution, called **brine**, rises to the surface. This solution is used to make table salt. It is also to make other products such as those shown in the table and photographs.

Product	Uses
bleach	household cleaners; disinfectants
chlorine	swimming pools; water supplies
hydrogen	to make ammonia; to make margarine
sodium hydroxide	oven cleaner; to unblock sinks

Bottles of bleach and toilet cleaner.

c Chlorine is a very poisonous gas. It was used as a weapon in the First World War. How can chlorine safely be used in swimming pools?

Testing for salt

We can test for both sodium and chloride in sodium chloride.

Sodium can be identified using the flame test. A sample of the salt is brought into a very hot Bunsen flame using a piece of flame test wire. The bright yellow flame shows sodium is present.

To test for chloride, a few drops of silver nitrate solution are added to a solution you think may be a chloride. If chloride ions are present, the solution goes cloudy white.

TASKS

1 The sea contains dissolved sodium chloride. In some countries with hot climates salt is obtained from sea water. Suggest how this is done.

2 In Utah in the USA there are vast salt flats. A thick bed of salt stretches for many miles. Salt flats were formed when land movements trapped parts of the sea. Suggest how these salt flats were formed from trapped sea water millions of years ago.
Portfolio Unit 3 b2

3.8 Making salt

The chemical name for 'common salt' is sodium chloride. There are two ways of making sodium chloride in the laboratory.

Direct combination

Sodium metal and chlorine gas can combine to make sodium chloride.

A small piece of sodium metal is heated in a Bunsen burner flame. When it is lowered into a gas jar filled with chlorine, the sodium metal and chlorine gas react violently. The sodium burns with a bright yellow light.

In the violent reaction, the elements sodium and chlorine combine to make the compound sodium chloride. This appears as a white powder on the sides of the gas jar.

$$\text{sodium} + \text{chlorine} \rightarrow \text{sodium chloride}$$
$$2Na + Cl_2 \rightarrow 2NaCl$$

Neutralisation

Sodium hydroxide and hydrochloric acid react to make sodium chloride.

$$\text{sodium hydroxide} + \text{hydrochloric acid} \rightarrow \text{sodium chloride} + \text{water}$$
$$NaOH + HCl \rightarrow NaCl + H_2O$$

This type of reaction between an alkali and an acid is called **neutralisation**. Whatever alkali and acid are used, a salt and water are produced. Sodium chloride is a salt but there are many other salts. Different alkalis and acids produce different salts.

a Suggest why neutralisation is a safer way of making sodium chloride than direct combination.

It is important that exactly equal amounts of sodium hydroxide and hydrochloric acid are mixed together. In this way none of the alkali or acid will be left unreacted to contaminate the sodium chloride.

b Why might sodium chloride contaminated with acid or alkali be a bad idea?

When the neutralisation reaction has taken place a solution of sodium chloride is formed. **Crystals** can be prepared from this solution. Some of the water is evaporated off by boiling the solution. The more concentrated solution is then left to cool. White crystals of sodium chloride are formed.

c Sodium hydroxide and sulfuric acid react together in a neutralisation. A salt and water are produced. What is the name of this salt?

Uses of pure sodium chloride

As well as being used to flavour food, pure sodium chloride has other uses.

For centuries sodium chloride has been used to preserve food. Bacteria cannot grow in a high concentration of sodium chloride, so the food does not go bad. Fish and bacon are examples of salted food.

Pure sodium chloride is used to make sodium carbonate. This is used to make glass.

d Why must the salt used to preserve food and to make sodium carbonate be pure?

e Sodium chloride used for preserving food is made from rock salt or by **evaporation** of sea water. Why is direct combination or neutralisation not used to make this sodium chloride?

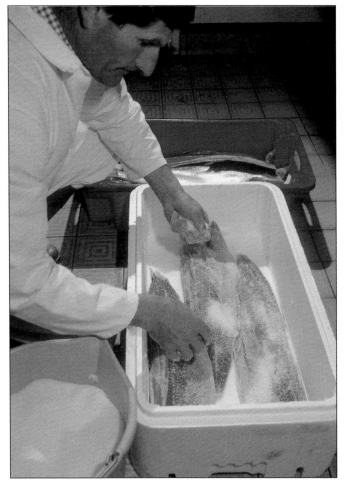
Salt being used to preserve fish.

TASKS

1 Suggest what safety precautions should be taken for each of the two methods of preparing salt described in this section: direct combination and neutralisation.
Portfolio Unit 1 a1, a2, a3

2 **Preparation of ammonium sulfate**
Portfolio Unit 1, Unit 3

3 **Indigestion tablets**
Portfolio Unit 1, Unit 3

 **More questions**

3.9 Chrome yellow

No parking!

When you walk through any city centre you see yellow lines on most of the roads. The lines show where motorists are not allowed to park their cars.

a Suggest why this yellow is used for the lines which show where cars cannot be parked.

The yellow colour for these lines is due to a **pigment** called lead chromate or chrome yellow. It is the same pigment that van Gogh used in his sunflower paintings.

Making lead chromate

Solutions of lead nitrate and sodium chromate mixed together make lead chromate. A deep yellow solid is formed. A solid that is formed when two solutions are mixed together is called a **precipitate**. The correct description for our solid is a yellow precipitate.

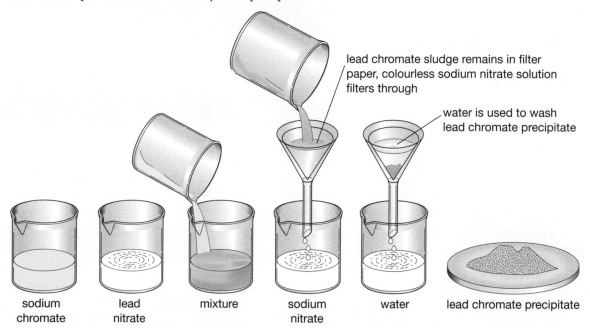

lead chromate sludge remains in filter paper, colourless sodium nitrate solution filters through

water is used to wash lead chromate precipitate

| sodium chromate | lead nitrate | mixture | sodium nitrate | water | lead chromate precipitate |

sodium chromate + lead nitrate → lead chromate + sodium nitrate

Great care has to be taken when lead chromate is made. It is very poisonous and may cause a range of effects, including kidney damage, impaired eyesight, nerve damage and cancer.

b Suggest what simple safety precautions are taken when lead chromate is made.

c Why is lead chromate paint not used to paint toys for young children?

How much lead chromate can be made?

In theory 1.0 kg of lead nitrate makes 1.2 kg of lead chromate. This is called the theoretical **yield**. However, you are likely to make less than this because some of the mass remains on the equipment, such as the beakers. The mass you make is called the actual yield.

d **Look back at how lead chromate is made. Where are you likely to lose some of the lead chromate?**

Suppose you make 0.9 kg of lead chromate from 1.0 kg of lead nitrate. You can calculate the percentage yield.

$$\text{percentage yield} = \frac{\text{actual yield}}{\text{theoretical yield}} \times 100$$
$$= \frac{0.9}{1.2} \times 100$$
$$= 75\%$$

e **In another experiment 1.2 kg of lead chromate is made from 2.0 kg of lead nitrate. What is the percentage yield?**

f **Why do manufacturers need to know the percentage yield of the chemical they are making?**

H More on yield CD-ROM

TASKS

1 A **precipitation** reaction (like the reaction that makes lead chromate) is a reaction where two solutions mixed together make an insoluble solid.

If you mix solutions of barium chloride and sodium sulfate together, you make barium sulfate. This is a precipitation reaction because barium sulfate is an insoluble solid.

a Write the word equation for the barium chloride/sodium sulfate reaction.

b Copy and complete the symbol equation. Use the table on page 211 to help you.

__________ + __________ → __________ + 2__________

c 8 g of barium chloride should produce a theoretical yield of 10 g of barium sulfate. In an experiment 7 g of barium sulfate is produced. Calculate the percentage yield of barium sulfate.

Portfolio Unit 3 b2

2 Preparation of barium sulfate CD-ROM

Portfolio Unit 1, Unit 3

3 Preparation of silver chloride CD-ROM

Portfolio Unit 1, Unit 3

3.10 Ammonium sulfate

Fertilisers

Plants need a supply of nitrogen to grow. Although there is plenty of nitrogen gas in the air, plants cannot use this supply. Plants get the nitrogen they need by taking in nitrates in solution through their roots.

When crops are grown repeatedly in the same field, the supply of nitrogen in the soil is quickly used up. Unless the farmer puts more nitrogen back into the soil, the growth of future crops will be poor.

Farmers use **fertilisers** to put nitrogen back into the soil. (Also see Chapter 1.)

Spreading fertiliser.

a Suggest why farmers in underdeveloped countries may not spread fertilisers on their soil.

A number of compounds can be used as fertilisers, including ammonium nitrate and ammonium sulfate.

Making ammonium sulfate and ammonium nitrate

A neutralisation reaction is used to make ammonium sulfate.

In industry, ammonium sulfate is made from reacting the chemicals ammonia and sulfuric acid together.

b Write a word equation for the reaction producing ammonium sulfate in industry.

In the laboratory, ammonium sulfate is made when ammonium hydroxide solution is neutralised by sulfuric acid:

ammonium hydroxide + sulfuric acid → ammonium sulfate + water

c Suggest how crystals of ammonium sulfate can be obtained from the solution produced in this reaction.

Ammonium nitrate is made from reacting two chemicals in large amounts.

d Which two chemicals would be used in industry to form ammonium nitrate?

Relative formula mass

Ammonium nitrate has the formula NH_4NO_3. An atom of each element in this formula has a mass called the **relative atomic mass**. If we add the relative atomic masses of all the atoms in the formula together, we get the relative formula mass for the compound.

Element	Name of atoms	Relative atomic mass	Total mass of element
N	2	14	28
H	4	1	4
O	3	16	48
relative formulae mass of NH_4NO_3 =			80

a Work out the relative formula mass for ammonia gas, NH_3, and for water, H_2O.

Ammonium nitrate explosion

On Friday 21 September 2001 a huge explosion ripped through the AZT fertiliser factory at Toulouse, France. The explosion occurred in a warehouse in which granular ammonium nitrate was stored. The blast blew out windows in the city centre 3 km away and created a crater 50 m wide and 10 m deep.

Under normal conditions ammonium nitrate does not pose any risks, but if heated to between 160°C and 200°C it can cause an explosion. It is estimated that between 200 and 300 tonnes of ammonium nitrate blew up at the factory.

The cause of the explosion is unknown. The factory normally has about 6300 tonnes of liquefied ammonia and 6000 tonnes of solid ammonium nitrate and 30 000 tonnes of solid fertiliser on the site.

e Suggest what precautions should be taken when storing ammonium nitrate.

f A chemist suggested that an electrical fault in the building caused a fire that led to this explosion. What information in the paragraphs above supports this idea?

g What other dangers to people living locally might be caused by an explosion at this factory?

 **Making ammonia**

TASKS

1 Both ammonium sulfate and ammonium nitrate may be used as fertilisers.
Design an experiment to find out which of these two compounds is the better fertiliser.
Portfolio Unit 1 c2

2 **Preparation of ammonium sulfate**
Portfolio Unit 1, Unit 3

3.11 Bulk and fine chemicals

The chemical industry

The chemical industry manufactures a wide range of materials. Some materials are used as ingredients for products sold directly to the public, for example paints, deodorants and washing powders. Other materials are bought by other manufacturers to make their products. Total sales of chemicals in the United Kingdom are over £35 billion each year.

Bulk chemicals

Some chemicals are used in very large quantities. These include sulfuric acid, ammonia and polythene. These materials are called **bulk chemicals**.

Bulk chemicals have to be transported around the country. Most are taken by road. This road tanker is delivering sulfuric acid to a customer.

Many bulk chemicals are **corrosive** or **poisonous** and are therefore **hazardous** to transport. Great care has to be taken to protect road users from dangerous chemicals.

Fine chemicals

Some materials are produced in much smaller quantities than bulk chemicals. Examples are medicines, dyes and pigments. These are called **fine chemicals** or speciality chemicals. Fine chemicals are usually more expensive than bulk chemicals.

a Suggest why fine chemicals are more expensive than bulk chemicals.

The work of scientists

Scientists have many different jobs in the chemical industry. The table gives information about some of these jobs.

Scientists testing polluted water.

Job title	What the scientist does
Research chemist	Discovers new chemicals and finds out how they can be used
Chemical engineer	Designs and runs a factory used to manufacture useful chemicals
Quality control chemist	Tests chemicals before they are sold to make sure that they are the correct mixture, concentration, etc
Environmental scientist	Assesses impact of chemicals on the environment

A biomedical engineer at work

H More on bulk and fine chemicals CD-ROM

TASKS

1 About 14% of the United Kingdom's chemical production takes place in Yorkshire and Humberside, an area in the North-east of England.

The list shows some of the chemicals produced in this area.

dyes
fertiliser
paints
pesticides
pharmaceuticals (medicines and drugs)
pigments
plastics, e.g. polythene
textile fibres, e.g. nylon

a Divide this list into two new lists, one of bulk chemicals and one of fine chemicals.
b Try to find out what chemical industries are in your nearest industrial area. What do they produce? Are they mainly bulk chemicals or fine chemicals?

Portfolio Unit 3 a2

3.12 Making metals

Occurrence and extraction of metals

Most metals are found as **ores**. An ore is a mixture of a metal or a metal compound with rocks.

Some metals are found uncombined with other elements. These are metals with very low reactivity. The metal simply has to be separated from the rocks in which it is found. Gold is such a metal.

Other more reactive metals are found as metal compounds. Iron is usually found as iron oxide and lead is usually found as lead sulfide. These metals need to be extracted from their ores by chemical means.

Reducing iron oxide to iron in a blast furnace.

Metal ores

A common ore of iron is haematite, which contains iron oxide. Galena is an ore containing lead sulfide.

a Some metals, such as gold, are found as the metal in an ore, not a metal compound. Other ores, such as iron and zinc, are found as metal compounds. Explain the difference.

To get iron from haematite the ore is mixed with carbon and heated. The carbon removes the oxygen from the iron oxide, leaving iron metal.

$$iron\ oxide + carbon \rightarrow iron + carbon\ dioxide$$
$$2Fe_2O_3 + 3C \rightarrow 4Fe + 3CO_2$$

The iron oxide is being reduced in this reaction. Oxygen is removed from it. This is called **reduction**.

To get lead from galena the ore is first roasted in air to convert the lead sulfide to lead oxide. Then lead oxide is reduced with carbon to form lead metal.

$$lead\ oxide + carbon \rightarrow lead + carbon\ monoxide$$

b Explain what is meant by the word 'reduction'.

Haematite that has been partly polished.

Environmental impact

The extraction of metals from their ores can cause pollution of the environment.

Scientists work to reduce the environmental impact of metal extraction to a minimum.

Waste gases from metal extraction methods contain fine dust particles, which come from the ore and other materials used in the extraction. The waste gases are passed through 'scrubbers' to remove these dust particles.

Poisonous gases such as carbon monoxide are not released into the environment. Carbon monoxide is flammable. It is burned as a fuel, making carbon dioxide which is not poisonous. The heat produced in the reaction is used in the metal extraction process. This protects the environment in two ways, since it saves using so much fossil fuel.

In some extraction processes water is used. This can become contaminated with poisonous metal compounds. The water is purified by removal of these compounds before it is released into a river.

c   Explain how burning the carbon monoxide in waste gases helps the environment in two different ways.

Polluted land around a metal extraction site

TASKS

1   The table gives information about some metal ores.

Name of main ore	Formula of metal compound in main ore	Annual world production/ 1000 tonnes (1986)	Price per tonne (1987)	Main uses of metal
copper pyrites	CuS	7500	£940	wires, pipes, alloys
haematite	Fe_2O_3	710 000	£130	steel, vehicles, tools, engines
galena	PbS	4000	£300	roofing, solder, batteries
tinstone	SnO_2	133	£4500	'tin' cans, solder, alloys
zinc blende	ZnS	5000	£475	galvanising, alloys

Use information from the table to answer the following questions.
a Which of the metals in the list is most used in the world?
b Which ore would you use to extract tin?
c Which two metals are used in solder?
d Which is the most expensive metal in the table? Suggest why.
e Which ores would need to be roasted in air before reduction with carbon?

Portfolio Unit 3 d2

Case Study: A road tanker accident

Tom is a fire fighter. One of his jobs is to help at the scene of road accidents.

On an icy winter morning Tom is called to an accident. A road tanker skidded and hit a river bridge. The tanker overturned, spilling a liquid chemical over the road. Police closed the road and called the fire brigade.

Before the fire fighters start to clear up the accident, they need to know what the chemical is and how to treat it.
Tom looks at the hazard warning symbol on a sign at the back of the tanker.

What hazard?

The sign also says that the tanker is carrying sulfuric acid.

Tom and the other fire fighters then use the hoses on their fire engine to wash the acid away.

Assessing environmental damage

Some of the sulfuric acid may have washed into the river. The river contains many different species of aquatic plant, and is the habitat of animals such as fish and water voles.

An environmental scientist is called to the scene to find out if the river has been polluted by the acid.

barium nitrate solution   sample from river

Sulfuric acid, H_2SO_4, or salts containing sulfate, such as sodium sulfate, Na_2SO_4, can be tested for the sulfate ion SO_4^{2-}.

Barium nitrate solution is added to the suspected sulfate solution. A white cloudy precipitate in the solution would prove that sulfate is present.

The environmental scientist has a test tube containing a sample of water from the river and a test tube containing barium nitrate solution. He mixes the two liquids.

1 Why did the police close the road at the scene of this accident?

2 Why does the sulfuric acid need to be washed off the road?

3 What precautions should the fire fighters take?

4 Does the test carried out by the environmental scientist show that the acid has washed into the river?

5 How might this pollution problem be solved?

white cloudy precipitate

1 Sea water contains sodium chloride as well as some other dissolved chemicals. You can buy 'sea salt' from the supermarket. Some people add sea salt to their food because they prefer the taste of sea salt to that of table salt, which is pure sodium chloride.

    a How could you get solid sea salt from sea water? [2]

    b Suggest why sea salt may taste different from table salt. [1]

2 Here is a list of the fractions obtained from crude oil.

    bitumen, diesel, fuel oil, kerosene, LPG, naphtha, petrol

    a What physical property of the chemicals in these fractions enables them to be separated? [1]

    b More of the petrol fraction is used than any other. Suggest why. [1]

    c Additional petrol can be made from naphtha. Why may this use of naphtha cause problems in the future? [1]

3 The table shows the chemical formulae of some substances.

Substance	Formula
ammonia	NH_3
ammonium sulfate	$(NH_4)_2SO_4$
argon	Ar
chlorine	Cl_2
copper	Cu
sodium chloride	$NaCl$
sodium carbonate	Na_2CO_3

    a Which substance is an element made of molecules? [1]

    b Which substance is a compound of a metal and a non-metal? [1]

    c Which substance is a gas made from individual atoms? [1]

    d How many elements are in the compound ammonium sulfate? [1]

    e How many atoms are in the formula of sodium carbonate? [1]

4 The sentences below give instructions for the separation of pure sodium chloride from rock salt. The problem is that the instructions are in the wrong order. Re-arrange the sentences into the correct order.

    A Filter the mixture and collect the filtrate.

    B Stir the rock salt in warm water.

    C Filter off the crystals.

    D Leave the saturated solution to cool.

    E Evaporate the filtrate to half volume. [4]

5 Gold is a very unreactive metal. Use this idea to explain the following facts about gold.

    a Gold is used for jewellery. [1]

    b Gold is found in the ground as the element. [1]

6 Sulfur is also found as the element. Describe three differences between gold and sulfur. [3]

7 The list shows the names of the three sub-atomic particles:
- electron
- neutron
- proton.

a Which particle is **not** found in the nucleus of an atom? [1]

b Which particle has very little mass? [1]

c Which particle has no charge? [1]

8 A green solid is added to dilute hydrochloric acid. It gives off a gas that turns limewater milky. A sample of the substance gives a green colour to a Bunsen burner flame.

a Name the substance. [2]

b Explain how you worked out this name. [2]

9 a Calcium carbonate decomposes when it is heated. Complete the equation for the reaction.

calcium carbonate → calcium oxide + _____ _____ [2]

b When calcium oxide is added to water a strongly exothermic reaction takes place. Complete this symbol equation for the reaction.

$CaO + H_2O \rightarrow$ _____ [2]

10 Limestone is made of calcium carbonate. Acid rain contains sulfuric acid. Limestone is attacked by acid rain.

a What is the cause of acid rain? [2]

b Write a word equation for the reaction between limestone and acid rain. [2]

11 Marble is made of calcium carbonate. Marble reacts with hydrochloric acid.

a The reaction is faster if small marble chippings are used instead of large ones. Explain why. [1]

b State two other ways in which this reaction could be speeded up. [2]

12 The table shows the formulae of some compounds.

Compound	Formula
A	H—C—C—H (with H atoms above and below each C)
B	(HO)₂S with two O double bonds
C	H₂C=CH₂
D	H—C—C—OH (with H atoms, ethanol structure)

a Which two compounds are hydrocarbons? [1]

b Which compound is inorganic? [1]

c Which compound has the formula C_2H_6? [1]

13 This word equation shows a reaction between an acid and an alkali.

potassium hydroxide + hydrochloric acid → potassium chloride + water

a Which substance is the alkali? [1]

b What type of reaction is this? [1]

c What is always formed in this type of reaction? [1]

d How can you show that the product of this reaction is a chloride? [2]

e What would be the products of a reaction between potassium hydroxide and sulfuric acid? [2]

14 Here is a list of substances. Re-arrange the list into three lists to show which of the substances are elements, which are compounds and which are mixtures.
**zinc   sodium chloride   phosphorus
sea water   iodine   carbon dioxide
oxygen   wood   calcium carbonate
air   nitrogen   argon
carbon tetrachloride   ethanol
strontium   copper sulfate
lithium chlorine   milk   lead nitrate
polythene   crude oil**   [22]

15 Here are some relative atomic masses:
hydrogen H = 1, potassium K = 39,
nitrogen N = 14, sodium Na = 23,
oxygen O = 16, zinc Zn = 65.
Use these to work out the relative formula masses of the following compounds:
zinc oxide ZnO, sodium chloride NaCl,
potassium hydroxide KOH,
sodium nitrate $NaNO_3$, potassium sulfate
K_2SO_4, zinc nitrate $Zn(NO_3)_2$.   [6]

16 When a solution of barium nitrate is added to a solution of sodium sulfate, a white precipitate of barium sulfate is formed.
a Write a word equation for this reaction.   [2]
b Describe how you would get pure, dry barium sulfate from this reaction.   [3]

17 Sodium nitrate can be used as a fertiliser. Sodium nitrate can be made by the reaction of an acid with an alkali.
a What name is given to the reaction between an acid and an alkali?   [2]
b Name the acid and alkali that can be used to make sodium nitrate.   [2]
c Write a word equation for the reaction.   [2]
d Describe how you would use this reaction to make crystals of sodium nitrate.   [2]

18 Sulfuric acid and ammonium nitrate are bulk chemicals. Aspirin and penicillin are fine chemicals. Use these examples to explain the difference between bulk and fine chemicals.   [2]

19 Iron is made from an iron ore called haematite.
a Iron ore contains about 80% iron oxide, Fe_2O_3. How is the oxygen removed from iron oxide to get iron metal?   [2]
b Another iron ore, called iron pyrites, contains iron sulfide. What must be done to this ore before it can be used to make iron metal?   [1]
c Some metal ores contain only a small percentage of the metal compound. What must be done to these ores before the metal can be extracted?   [1]

123

Case study: Fitting double-glazed windows

Neil and his dad fit double-glazed windows.

Mostly they replace old wooden window frames with new ones made of uPVC. Wooden window frames need to be painted or stained. After years of bad weather, wooden window frames rot.

The new uPVC window frames do not rot because uPVC is not biodegradable. The new frames are available in white or other colours, and never need painting.

The old wooden frames can be disposed of by burning. If uPVC is burned it gives off poisonous fumes. If old uPVC frames are not burned they are put into landfill sites, where they will stay for hundreds of years.

uPVC is made using chemicals from crude oil. Wood comes from trees. Neil tells his father that they should use new wooden frames because wood is more sustainable than uPVC.

When Neil and his dad fit a window frame, Neil fills the gaps around each frame by using expanded polyurethane foam. Polyurethane is a polymer. When it is squirted from a pressured can into the gaps around the window frame, bubbles of gas expand in the polymer creating a colloid called a foam.

When the polyurethane has set hard, excess foam can be cut away with a knife. The foam is a composite, made of two materials – polyurethane and gas. It is strong and light, ideal for holding the window frame in place. Neil then fixes uPVC trim around the frame to give a neat finish.

1 Describe two advantages of uPVC window frames compared with wooden frames.

2 Describe two disadvantages of uPVC window frames compared with wooden frames.

3 Neil says that he and his dad should fit wooden frames instead of uPVC.

   Explain why Neil may be correct.

4 Why is expanded polyurethane foam a good material to fill gaps around window frames?

How this chapter can help you with your portfolio

Unit I

● You can look at the health and safety issues involved in a school pottery class. Your CD-ROM contains information about health and safety rules to help you.

The things that you use every day in your kitchen are made from different materials. Each type of material has properties that make it ideal for certain uses.

Metals

Some of the articles in your kitchen are made from metals. **Metals** are good **conductors** of heat. This means that heat passes through them quickly. Metals can be rigid, like kettles, or bendy, like wire. Metals are hard and do not break easily but can be quite heavy.

These are made of metal.

a You can also have plastic knives. How are metal knives better than plastic knives?

Plastics

Lots of things in your house are made from plastics or **polymers**. Polymers are lighter and can also be more flexible than metals. They are the ideal material for plastic shopping bags, which need to be light and bendy but also need to be very strong. But there are many different kinds of polymer.

These are made of plastics.

Many polymers melt much more easily than metals. Have you ever left a CD or vinyl record on a car parcel shelf on a sunny day? They soon start to soften and bend out of shape.

Some other polymers do not melt easily. Many kettles and toasters now have bodies made of hard polymers that can stand heat. Also, since polymers do not conduct heat as well as metals, the kettles and toasters never become too hot to touch.

b Why is a kettle body not made from the same polymer as a plastic bag?

c Why is a plastic electric kettle safer than a metal one?

Ceramics

Plates, cups and mugs are usually made from pottery or china. These are **ceramic** materials.

Ceramics are bad conductors of heat. This means the coffee in your mug can be steaming hot but the handle will still be cool enough to hold. Ceramics are hard and strong, but break easily if they are dropped.

These are made of ceramic.

d Why are coffee mugs made of ceramics rather than metal?

e People going camping usually take plastic plates and mugs. Why do you think this is?

Composites

Sometimes two materials are combined to make one material, called a **composite** material. The composite material uses the properties of both of them.

The sports car in this photograph has a body made from fibreglass. This is a mixture of a polymer and glass. Fibreglass is light and strong. The glass fibres give strength to the polymer. Fibreglass is an example of a material called glass-reinforced plastic (GRP).

The body of this car is made of a composite material.

f Why might it be dangerous to make a car body from polymer that is not mixed with glass fibres?

TASKS

1 Copy the table. Use the information on these pages to fill in the properties of metals, polymers and ceramics. Answer either 'yes' or 'no'.

	Metal	Polymer	Ceramic
Does it conduct heat?			
Does it break easily?			
Can it be flexible?			
Can it be heavy?			

2 Stephen is setting up a catering company. He is already planning to cater for

• a children's party
• a wedding
• a picnic.

For each event, suggest what materials Stephen will need for
a plates
b packaging
c cups.
Explain all your choices.
Portfolio Unit 3 a1

4.2 Metals

The photograph shows a building being built. The builders are using wooden scaffolding.

Scaffolding has to be
- strong
- rigid and not bend
- easy to join.

a Why is metal scaffolding better than wood scaffolding?

Metals have properties that make them useful for many things.

Copper is a metal with a large number of uses. It can be drawn into fine wires. It can also be beaten into sheets, that is, it is **malleable**. It is a good conductor of electricity.

The photographs show copper being used for electrical wiring and for a copper roof.

b Make a list of the properties of copper that make it useful for each of the uses shown in photographs 1 and 2.

Properties of metals

Most metals have the same useful properties as copper.
- They are good conductors of electricity.
- They are malleable, i.e. they can be beaten into sheets.
- They can be drawn into fine wires.
- They are hard.

We choose metals with the correct properties to do particular jobs.

We would not make a bicycle frame from lead because it is too heavy and not strong enough.

The table shows properties of some metals and the uses that depend on these properties.

Metal	Property	Use
iron (steel)	hard and tough	car bodies
copper	good conductor of electricity	electrical wiring
copper	good conductor of heat	saucepans
aluminium	resistant to corrosion	greenhouse and window frames
aluminium (alloy)	low density	aeroplane bodies

Recycling metals

A mixture of metals is called an **alloy**. When metals are mixed together their properties change, making the alloy more useful for some jobs than the metals on their own.

Metals can be recycled. This is worth doing if the cost of recycling is less than the cost of extracting the metal. Iron (steel) and aluminium are two of the most commonly recycled metals.

The recycling of metals has advantages and disadvantages.

Aluminium cans for recycling.

Advantages	Disadvantages
It may cost less to recycle than extract more metal	Scrap metal has to be collected
It saves valuable resources	The metal has to be sorted from other materials
It may cause less damage to the environment	For metals used in small quantities it may be difficult to collect enough to recycle
Recycling uses less energy than extraction	Recycling often depends on the public to separate metal from other rubbish
Less metal is dumped to poison the environment	

c Suggest why not all metals are recycled.

More on metals CD-ROM

TASKS

1 The photograph shows overhead power cables.

Overhead power cables must
- carry electricity well
- be as light as possible
- not rust.

Choose a metal from the table to use for overhead power cables.

Explain your choice.

Metal	How tough is it?	How heavy is it?	How good is it at conducting electricty	Does it rust?
pure aluminium	not tough	light	very good	no
aluminium alloy	tough	light	good	no
copper	not tough	very heavy	very good	no
steel	tough	heavy	good	yes

Portfolio Unit 3 c1

The uses of polythene

The plastic carrier bags provided by many shops are made from the polymer poly(ethene), often called polythene.

a A large supermarket uses thousands of polythene carrier bags each day. What does this suggest about the cost of polythene?

Many of the products you can buy from supermarkets are in polythene containers. These range from loaves of bread in polythene bags to washing-up liquid in polythene bottles.

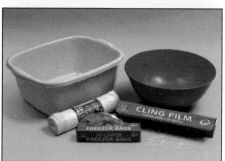

b What do you think could have been used to wrap sandwiches before polythene was invented?

c All the products in the picture are made from polythene. Can you name all the products?

Properties of polythene

Like most polymers, polythene is made from the chemicals in crude oil.

Polythene is a good material for many household articles because it is **flexible**. This means that polythene will bend without breaking. Polythene is also tough and water resistant.

Another property of polythene is that it melts at a low temperature. This makes it easy for factories to form it into thin sheets for bags or into the shape of bowls and bottles.

d Polythene does not become brittle at very low temperatures. Why is this a useful property?

There is another form of polythene, which is much harder and less flexible than the polythene used to make plastic bags. This other form of polythene also melts at a higher temperature. It has different properties from normal polythene because it is made in a different way. This harder polythene is used for milk crates and water pipes.

Nylon

In the 1940s 'nylons' became an essential item of clothing for women. They were made from the polymer nylon, which is still used to make modern 'tights'. Nylon fibres are very flexible, and can be woven to make clothing and carpets. It is tough and hard-wearing. Nylon bristles are used in toothbrushes and brooms. Like polythene, nylon melts easily when heated.

PVC and other polymers

PVC is another polymer. PVC is flexible and melts easily. It is used to make many articles, including gutters, drainpipes and CDs.

The kettle in the photograph is made from a polymer called PEEK. This polymer is strong and will not melt when the water boils. Melamine is another polymer that has a high melting point. It is used to make kitchen work surfaces.

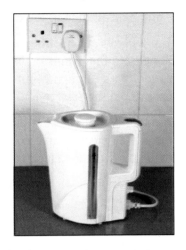

e Why would the type of polythene used to make plastic bottles be a bad choice of material for the body of an electric kettle?

Some polymers are very strong. Police officers and soldiers wear protective vests made from the polymer Kevlar. Kevlar is light in weight but may stop a bullet or knife injuring the police officer or soldier. These photographs show the protection worn by a medieval knight and a modern police officer.

f What material is the knight's armour made from?

g What advantages does Kevlar have over this material in protecting a modern police officer?

More on polymers CD-ROM

Ancient and modern.

TASKS

1 Uses for polymers include the following articles:

- carrier bags
- a plastic-bodied kettle
- soft drink bottles
- guttering and drainpipes
- a police officer's protective vest
- milk crates.

For each of these articles, answer the following questions.

a What other material could be used to make this article?

b What advantage does the polymer have over this other material?

Portfolio Unit 3 a1

More questions CD-ROM

4.4 Ceramics

The electricity passing through these power cables is at 110 000 volts, but you will not get electrocuted if you stand beneath one of the pylons.

You will not get electrocuted because the power cables hang from the pylons on ceramic insulators. Electricity cannot pass through ceramic materials so it cannot pass down the steel pylon to the ground.

A material that does not allow electricity to pass through it is called an electrical **insulator**. Ceramic materials are good electrical insulators.

Fired clay

Ceramic articles are made from clay, similar to the clay you could dig up in a garden. Clay is soft and easy to mould into shape when it is wet. As it dries it becomes hard, but it is still very easily broken. After it is fired in a hot oven, called a kiln, it becomes very hard and strong. It is still **brittle**, and will break if dropped.

We have uncovered human-made ceramics that date back to at least 24 000 BC – that's about 26 000 years ago!

a Suggest what prehistoric people may have used ceramic materials for.

Different coloured glazes can be used, so ceramic articles can be made in many different colours and with patterns or paintings on them.

Properties of ceramics

Ceramic materials have many useful properties. They are

- hard
- strong
- easy to clean
- heat resistant
- good electrical insulators
- and they do not react easily with chemicals.

You will probably have many ceramic articles in your house, including cups, plates, toilets and wall tiles.

b What advantages do ceramic materials have for making a toilet?

Using ceramics

Ceramic materials are used in many other places.

For example, dentists use ceramics for tooth replacements and braces.

c Why are ceramic materials good for tooth replacements?

Clay bricks are used to build homes, offices and factories because of their strength, **durability** and beauty. Brick is the only building product that will not burn, melt, dent, peel, warp, rot, rust or be eaten by termites.

d What other materials can you build a house from?

e Why are these materials not as good as bricks?

Glass and cement are more examples of ceramics. Glass is used for windows because it is **transparent**, has a low density and is hard. Unfortunately, glass is also brittle.

 **More on giant structures**

TASKS

1 Here is a list of articles made from ceramic materials:

   roofing tile
   teapot
   kitchen floor tile
   porcelain ornament
   bathroom washbasin
   dinner plate.

   For each article answer the following questions.

   a What is the article used for?
   b What property of ceramic material makes it good for this article?
   c What other material could you use for this article?
   d Why would the ceramic material be better?

   Portfolio Unit 3 a1

2 Find out about the health and safety rules for using kilns and making pottery at school.
   You could ask your Art teacher or your Design and Technology teacher.
   List some of the rules and explain how they make the classroom a safer place to work.

   Portfolio Unit 1 a1

Modern sports equipment is often made from composite materials. A **composite material** is a mixture of two different materials. Good quality surfboards, mountain bikes and tennis racquets are made mainly from a mixture of glass or carbon fibres and a polymer resin. These have the useful properties of being light and strong, and also are not damaged by contact with water.

a Surfboards used to be made from wood. Why is a composite glass fibre or carbon fibre surfboard better than a wooden one?

b Most bicycle frames are made of steel. Some are made from aluminium alloy. What advantage does a carbon fibre frame have over frames made from these traditional materials?

The polymer PVC is a **rigid** material. It is suitable for making articles such as CDs. When **plasticisers** are added to PVC the composite material is much softer and more flexible. Plasticised PVC can be used as a cheap substitute for leather in the manufacture of briefcases and furniture.

A quick look at trainers

Trainers are made from a number of different materials. The uppers in many trainers are made partly of leather or PVC and partly of nylon or polyester. Leather and PVC are waterproof. Nylon and polyester allow water to pass through the fabric.

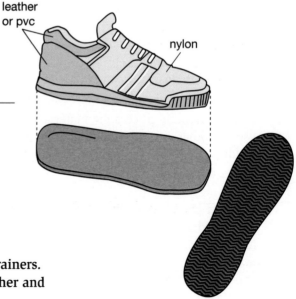

leather or pvc

nylon

c Your feet may sweat while you are wearing trainers. Why is it better to make the uppers from leather and polyester instead of just leather?

The soles of most trainers are made of a composite material. This is a polymer containing a plasticiser. The soles need to be tough and durable but also need to be flexible.

d Why is plasticiser added to the polymer that is used to make the soles of trainers?

Often the sole of a trainer also contains plasticised polyurethane foam. This is a polymer containing many small holes filled with air. Polyurethane foam is soft and spongy.

e Joggers wear trainers. Why would it be an advantage for the soles of these trainers to contain polyurethane foam?

Steel-reinforced concrete

Steel-reinforced concrete is a composite material widely used in the construction of buildings. Concrete is strong but not very flexible. Concrete slurry is poured around steel rods or mesh. When the concrete sets hard, the composite material is both strong and flexible, combining the properties of both concrete and steel.

 **More on composites**

TASKS

1 Cricket bats are traditionally made using wood from a willow tree.

Imagine that you are working for a company that makes cricket bats. Write a short note to your boss to convince him that your company should start making cricket bats from a composite material such as carbon fibre. You should compare the properties of both materials and their usefulness for making cricket bats. The table gives some information about the properties of willow and carbon fibre.

	Availability	Density	Water resistance	Strength	Flexibility
willow	renewable resource	medium	low, will warp or rot if wet	low	good
carbon fibre	non-renewable	very low	high	high	very good

Portfolio Unit 3 a2

 **More questions**

Your watch, your telephone and many of the products you use every day are made from many different materials.

Mobile phones and computers

Computers and mobile phones are made of many different materials. Each material has properties that make it suitable for a particular use.

The outer casing of these devices is plastic, made from a polymer such as ABS (acrylonitrile–butadiene–styrene). This material is strong, light in weight and easily moulded to make different shapes. ABS can also be coloured and even patterned.

a Explain how each of the five properties of ABS is a useful property for the casing of a mobile phone or computer.

Inside computers and mobile phones the components of the electrical circuits are connected on a circuit board. The connections between components are made using a metal such as copper. Copper conducts electricity well. On some circuit boards the connections are made using gold. Gold is a better electrical conductor than copper. At home you may have a set of stereo headphones with a gold plug.

b The wiring in a house is made from copper. Gold is a better conductor of electricity than copper. Why is house wiring not made from gold?

The small loudspeakers in mobile phones and in personal stereo earpieces are made using a ceramic material. The ceramic material vibrates to produce the sounds.

Developing new materials

New materials are continually being made to improve existing products or make new ones. For example, a new skateboard design may require a new type of glue to join together the layers of composite materials.

Scientists perform a number of jobs to help in the development of new materials:
- making the chemicals for new materials
- testing to find the properties of new materials
- matching new materials to their uses
- designing the manufacturing processes
- taking account of safety and environmental issues.

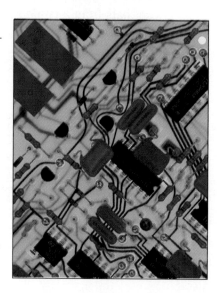

Motor cars

Many materials are used in a modern motor car. Fifty years ago wood was a common construction material used in cars.

c What are the disadvantages of using wood for the body or chassis of a car?

d Four types of material are mentioned on these two pages. What are these materials?

TASKS

1 The table shows some of the materials used in modern car manufacture. The table also shows some of the properties of the materials.

Material	Type of material	Properties
ABS	polymer	hard, very tough, will withstand minor impact without breaking, can be coloured
aluminium	metal	low density, strong, high melting point
copper	metal	good conductor of electricity, flexible
laminated glass	composite	transparent, strong, will not shatter into small pieces when broken
polyurethane foam	composite	fairly soft, will absorb energy when hit, can be coloured
porcelain	ceramic	good electrical insulator
PVC	polymer	soft, flexible, hard wearing, can be coloured and patterned
rubber	polymer	fairly soft, flexible, hard wearing
steel	metal	very strong, easily shaped, pieces can be welded together

This is a list of some car parts:
- body
- engine
- tyres
- bumpers
- exhaust pipe
- windscreen
- seats
- wiring
- dashboard (the part in front of the driver and the front seat passenger)
- spark plug (has a core to carry electrical current and an insulating body)

Suggest which material should be used for each part of the car in the list. Give reasons for each of your choices.

Portfolio Unit 3 a2, d2

137

The photograph shows a misty morning; but what is mist? Very small droplets of water are too light to fall to the ground. They are spread out through the air, forming mist.

a Why does mist usually form during the night?

Mist is an example of a material called a **colloid**. In a colloid, a substance in one state (solid, liquid or gas) is finely spread through a substance in another state. In this case the water, called the **disperse phase**, is spread through the air, called the **continuous phase**. Mist is a type of colloid called an **aerosol**.

b Suggest why mist soon disappears on a bright summer morning.

Different types of colloids

Many of the materials we use are colloids, for example shaving foam, aerosols and paint. Most dairy products such as milk, butter and cheese are colloids.

Colloids have different names according to the states of the disperse and continuous phases. An aerosol has a liquid dispersed in a gas. A **foam** has a gas dispersed in a liquid.

c Soaps and detergents form lather in water. Suggest what sort of colloid lather is.

We can also make a colloid from two liquids that do not mix. These liquids are said to be **immiscible**: Oil and water are one example.

Salad cream is a good example. It contains vinegar, one liquid, dispersed in oil, another liquid. Vinegar and oil do not dissolve in each other, so small droplets of the vinegar are spread out in the oil. This makes the colloid, called an **emulsion**. Wall paint is an emulsion. Milk is also an emulsion, containing fat droplets dispersed in water.

When butter is made from milk the two phases swap places. The solid fat is the continuous phase, with the liquid water dispersed in it. A colloid with a solid continuous phase and a liquid disperse phase is called a **gel**. Other examples are jelly and hair gel.

Not all mixtures of solids and liquids are colloids. When a substance such as salt is shaken with water, it dissolves to form a **solution**. This is transparent.

When a fine powder of an insoluble substance such as calcium carbonate is shaken with water, it forms a **suspension**. You cannot see through this mixture; it is opaque.

These foods are all colloids.

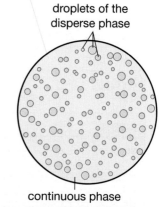

droplets of the disperse phase

continuous phase

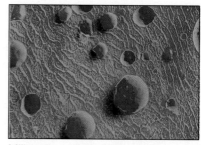

Milk cells under microscope.

Properties dictate uses

The properties of colloids make them useful.

- A *gel* is a thick semi-solid, so hair gel can be used to keep hair in place.
- An *emulsion* allows two liquids that would not normally mix to be kept together without separating out. The combination of vinegar and oil in salad cream gives the taste you want without the two liquids separating out in the bottle. Emulsions are also thick liquids. This makes emulsion paints easy to apply without the paint dripping.
- A *foam* keeps the gas mixed in with the liquid. Foam fire extinguishers use carbon dioxide gas dispersed in water. Carbon dioxide is not flammable, and helps to put out the fire. The foam does not collapse and so holds water over the fire. This helps to cool down the burning material.
- An *aerosol* has fine droplets of liquid dispersed in a gas. Aerosol sprays can be used in air fresheners to spread perfume through a room. This disguises nasty smells in the toilet or kitchen.

d When a razor is used to shave a man's face, water on the skin helps to lubricate the movement of the razor. This makes it easier to cut the hairs, without cutting the skin. Explain how the properties of shaving foam, which is an aerosol, help shaving.

TASKS

1 Different types of colloids are produced by the dispersion of different states. The table shows the names of these colloids and gives some examples.

Type of colloid	Continuous phase	Disperse phase	Example
–	gas	gas	–
aerosol	gas	liquid	mist, deodorant spray
aerosol	gas	solid	smoke
foam	liquid	gas	shaving cream
emulsion	liquid	liquid	salad cream, hand cream
sol	liquid	solid	paint, toothpaste
solid foam	solid	gas	pumice
solid emulsion	solid	liquid	butter, hair gel
solid sol	solid	solid	stained glass, gem stones

a When an egg white is whisked, air is forced into the liquid. What type of colloid is whisked egg white?

b Pumice is a type of rock sometimes formed when a volcano erupts. It is very light (low density). Explain why.

c Smoke and mist often look similar but they are quite different. Explain the difference between smoke and mist.

d Why is there no colloid with a gas dispersed in another gas?

Portfolio Unit 3 d2

4.8 Solid, liquid or gas?

Materials in the world around us exist mainly in three different *states*: solids (such as salt and copper sulfate), liquids (such as petrol and olive oil) and gases such the hydrogen used in an airship and the carbon dioxide used in some fire extinguishers.

The state of a material depends on how strongly the particles in the material are held together.
Forces called **bonds** act as 'glue' between the atoms.

There are two main types of bond: covalent and ionic.

Covalent bonds

Hydrogen is a gas. The atoms in hydrogen are joined to make pairs, called molecules, as H_2. In each molecule the atoms are joined by a **covalent bond**. In this bond two hydrogen atoms share a pair of electrons, one from each atom.

H—H

This covalent bond between two hydrogen atoms is very strong. It would therefore take a lot of energy to pull apart the two hydrogen atoms in a hydrogen molecule.

But the forces between different hydrogen molecules are very weak. It takes little energy to separate the hydrogen molecules from each other, so hydrogen turns into a gas at a very low temperature.

Covalent bonds are found in non-metal elements. Other examples are oxygen, nitrogen and chlorine, which are gases at room temperature.

a Why is oxygen not a liquid at room temperature?

Compounds with covalent bonds

In compounds of non-metals the atoms are held together by covalent bonds. A molecule of hydrogen chloride contains a hydrogen atom and a chlorine atom joined by a covalent bond. Although this covalent bond is very strong, the forces between different hydrogen chloride molecules are weak. Hydrogen chloride is a gas at room temperature.

Covalent compounds with small molecules are gases at room temperature.

Covalent compounds with larger molecules are liquids. Because the molecules are larger there are more forces between them, so more energy is needed to turn them into a gas. Most covalent compounds do not conduct electricity. Other examples of covalent compounds are carbon dioxide, ammonia and water.

Some covalent compounds have very large numbers of atoms joined to make one structure. These giant structures are solids with very high melting points. Examples are diamond and silicon dioxide.

b At room temperature carbon dioxide is a gas but silicon dioxide is a solid.
Explain why.

Ionic bonds

A compound between a metal atom and a non-metal atom has a different type of bond. This is an **ionic bond**. An example of ionic bonding is found in sodium chloride.

An electron from the sodium atom joins the chlorine atom. The sodium atom is now short of a negative electron, and so has a positive charge. The chlorine atom now has an extra negative electron, and so has a negative charge.

These positive and negative atoms are called **ions**. Attraction between the positive sodium ions and negative chloride ions holds them together in the ionic compound. This attraction is very strong, so a great deal of energy is needed to pull the ions apart. Sodium chloride is a solid at room temperature and has a high melting point.

Because ionic compounds contain charged particles, they conduct electricity when molten. Other examples of ionic compounds are magnesium oxide and copper sulfate.

c Petrol does not conduct electricity but molten sodium chloride does.
Explain why.

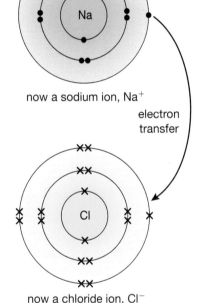

now a sodium ion, Na^+

electron transfer

now a chloride ion, Cl^-

H **More on chemical bonding** CD-ROM

TASKS

1 Write the names of the substances in this list under the headings 'Covalent Bonding' and 'Ionic Bonding'.

nitrogen, lithium chloride, fluorine, hydrogen bromide, potassium bromide, calcium oxide, copper chloride, carbon tetrachloride, sulfur dioxide

H **More questions** CD-ROM

Case Study: Laminate flooring

Katie wants to lay a new floor in her dining room. She visits a DIY store to look at flooring materials. The assistant shows her some laminate flooring. This is made of plastic, but is coloured to look like wood. The assistant says that it is more hard-wearing than wood, does not need to be stained or painted, and is easier to clean.

Katie discusses her new flooring with her friend Shaun. Shaun says that the plastic in laminate flooring is a polymer. This polymer is made from chemicals in crude oil. Shaun says that crude oil is a non-renewable material.

Shaun also tells Katie that the plastic in laminate flooring is not bio-degradable. He says that one day Katie will get fed up with the laminate flooring and want something else, or it will eventually wear out. When the flooring is taken up and thrown away it will cause pollution problems. It will either have to be dumped into a landfill site, where it will stay for hundreds of years, or burned, giving off poisonous fumes. Shaun advises Katie to use real wood for her new floor.

1 The laminate flooring is made form a non-renewable material. Why may this cause problems?

2 What other problems could be caused by using plastic laminate flooring?

3 Explain why wood may be a better material for Katie's floor.

4 In some ways plastic laminate flooring is better than wood. Suggest how.

1 The list shows a number of different materials. Copy the table and write the names of these materials in the correct columns.

**brick   concrete   copper   fibreglass
magnesium   plywood   poly(ethene)   porcelain**

Metals	Polymers	Ceramics	Composites

[8]

2 The list shows a number of articles. For each article suggest a suitable material and say why it is suitable for this article. Choose from these materials: ceramic, composite, metal, polymer.

**fishing rod   knife   saucepan   carrier bag
surfboard   teacup   washing-up bowl**   [7]

3 a What is meant by the term 'composite material'?   [1]

  b Why are composite materials often used instead of single materials?   [1]

  c Fibreglass is often used to make the bodies of sports cars. Most ordinary cars have bodies made of steel. Explain why fibreglass is a better choice for sports cars.   [1]

4 For each of the following uses, say which of the two metals is a better choice and why.

car bodies: lead or steel

electrical wires: copper or gold

jewellery: gold or steel

water pipes: copper or steel   [4]

5 The sentences below describe the making of pottery, but they are in the wrong order. Re-arrange the sentences into the correct order.

A The pot is fired in an oven.

B The surface of the pot is covered in a glaze.

C The pot is left to dry.

D Clay is dug up from the ground.

E The pot is fired again.

F The moist clay is shaped on a potters' wheel.   [5]

6 Copy this table and fill in the gaps to complete this information about colloids.

Type of colloid	Continuous phase	Disperse phase	Example
aerosol		liquid	mist, deodorant spray
aerosol	gas	solid	
	liquid	gas	shaving cream
emulsion	liquid		salad cream, hand cream
sol	liquid		paint, toothpaste
	solid	gas	pumice
solid emulsion	solid		butter, hair gel
solid sol		solid	stained glass, gemstones

[8]

7 House guttering used to be made from iron. Modern guttering is made from a polymer called PVC. Explain what advantages the polymer has over iron for this use. [3]

8 The polymer PEEK is used to make electric kettle bodies. The polymer Kevlar is used to make bullet-proof vests. Explain why each of these polymers is better than polythene for their particular use. [4]

9 Articles made from ceramic materials have been used for many thousands of years. Polymers have been used only in the past hundred years or so. Explain this difference. [2]

10 Most modern houses are built mainly of bricks. About 500 years ago most houses were made using a wooden frame. What are the advantages of using bricks for building houses? [3]

11 The polymer PVC is used to make rigid articles such as CDs. The same polymer can be used to make a very flexible material used as a cheaper substitute for leather. Explain how it is possible for PVC to be both rigid and flexible. [2]

12 Describe and explain why laminated car windscreens are much safer than those made from toughened glass. [4]

13 In the early part of the twentieth century fishing rods were made from bamboo canes. In the middle part of the twentieth century fibreglass was used. Modern fishing rods are made from carbon fibre.
  a Describe and explain the advantages gained from each change of material used to make fishing rods. [2]
  b What advantages does bamboo have over the other two materials? [2]

14 The following parts are needed for electricity cables to run between pylons:
  • cables between pylons
  • insulators between pylons and cables
  • legs of pylons.
  Suggest a suitable material for each part. Give reasons for your choices. [6]

15 A bicycle frame is usually made from one of three different materials:
  • aluminium alloy
  • carbon fibre
  • steel.
  Suggest the advantages and disadvantages of each material for making bicycles. [6]

16 A computer is made of many different materials. The list contains some of the parts in a computer:
  • circuit board
  • connections on circuit board
  • hard disk
  • outer casing.
  For each part, suggest a suitable material and give reasons for your choice. [8]

17 The wheels of horse-drawn carts were made of wood. Most modern cars have wheels made of steel and rubber.
  a Explain the advantages of using steel and rubber in wheel construction. [2]
  b Why could wood be used effectively for a cart but not for a motor car? [1]
  High-performance cars usually have wheel rims made from a magnesium alloy.
  c What advantages does magnesium alloy have over steel? [1]
  d Suggest why pure magnesium is not used to make wheel rims. [1]

18 The table gives information about some materials.

Material	Flexible?	Electrical conductor?	Melting point
A	no	yes	high
B	yes	no	low
C	no	no	high
D	no	no	low

Which material could be:
  a polythene [1]
  b porcelain [1]
  c copper [1]
  d PVC? [1]

19 Here are some metals and examples of
their use. For each, say why the metal is
good for its job.
aluminium: aeroplane bodies
copper: electrical wires
lead: deep sea divers' boots
steel: car bodies   [4]

20 Bleach and other household cleaners are
sold in polythene bottles. Explain why
polythene is a good material for containers
of these liquids.   [3]

21 Ben and Kelly want to have new double-
glazed windows fitted. Ben wants
windows with uPVC frames. Kelly wants
windows with wooden frames.
List the advantages and disadvantages of
using each of these materials for Ben and
Kelly's new window frames.   [4]

22 Many modern buildings are made using
steel-reinforced concrete. This is a
composite material.
  a What is the job of the steel in steel-
     reinforced concrete?   [1]
  b Why is concrete that is not reinforced
     with steel a poorer choice as a material
     for constructing a skyscraper?   [1]

23 The table shows how the materials used
to make certain articles have changed.

Article	Old material	New material
shopping bag	paper	polythene
car bumper	steel	ABS plastic
kettle	copper	PEEK polymer
tennis racquet	wood	carbon-reinforced fibreglass
stockings (tights)	silk	nylon
shoe soles	leather	plasticised polymer

For each article, say what advantages and
disadvantages the new material has when
compared with the old material.   [12]

24 Explain what is meant by the following
terms, when used to describe a colloid.
  a disperse phase   [2]
  b continuous phase   [2]

More questions CD-ROM

Case study: Plumbing and heating engineer

Eric is a plumbing and heating engineer. He has done this work since he left school. Like most plumbing and heating engineers, Eric is registered with **CORGI** (Council for Registered Gas Installers).

Eric has just taken out part of a gas fire to service it. He is looking at the area where the gas and air mix.

When the gas burns in a plentiful supply of oxygen, carbon dioxide and water are formed. But if there is not enough air, there is incomplete combustion and a poisonous gas, carbon monoxide, is formed instead.

The air for this gas fire comes into the house through an air vent. This passes under the floor and up through a grill into the room. Eric has found that the householder has put a plant trough in front of the air vent. Something as simple as this could lead to incomplete combustion and maybe the death of people in the house.

Every year up to 50 people die in the UK from carbon monoxide poisoning in their homes. Landlords who let flats must have gas appliances checked every year. Older central heating boilers have a balanced flue. This means that the air needed for the gas to burn is drawn in from outside and any waste gases are dispersed into the atmosphere.

New rules require gas boilers to have more ventilation, so modern boilers now have a fan as well.

1 What are the products of complete combustion?

2 What are the products of incomplete combustion?

3 Why is it important to have a gas appliance serviced regularly?

4 Why is it better to employ an engineer who is registered with CORGI?

5 What is the advantage of having a fan in the flue of a central heating boiler?

6 More deaths from carbon monoxide poisoning occur during winter months. Why is this?

How this chapter can help you with your portfolio

Unit 1

You can learn about radioactive materials. This will help you to understand some of the health and safety issues in one area of science and industry.

You will also learn about electrical circuits, electrical components, resistance and optical devices which will help you with these portfolio tasks:

- Aircraft construction
- Heater
- Components
- Starting blocks
- Camera

Unit 3

You can find out where different organisations are located and why.

You can also learn about work done and efficiency, which may help you with this portfolio task:

- Multigym

You may have seen pictures of oil fires burning.

This fire has been burning for nearly three months. During the 1991 Gulf War, there were many fires in the Kuwait oil fields. Oil is a **fossil fuel**. Fossil fuels are formed from the remains of animals and plants which have been compressed over millions of years.

Coal is also a fossil fuel.

So too is **natural gas**.

a Why are oil, coal and natural gas called fossil fuels?

You saw in Chapter 3 that crude oil is a mixture of hydrocarbons. Hydrocarbons are present in all fossil fuels.

b What two elements are present in all fossil fuels?

Fossil fuels are useful because they are concentrated sources of energy. When they are burned, energy is given out as heat. This heat is useful because it can keep us warm at home and give power stations the energy to make electricity.

When the fuels are burned, carbon dioxide and water are formed. This chemical equation shows what happens.

hydrocarbon + oxygen → carbon dioxide + water + energy

Coal

Although some people still cook food and heat their homes with coal, it is not the most common household fuel today. It is, however, one of the most efficient and economical fuels.

Homes heated by coal have better ventilation and there is always fresh air in the house. Medical research has shown that hay fever, asthma and eczema are reduced in homes with coal fires.

Coal has a lot of disadvantages. As well as being dirty, it does not burn away completely. Ash is left behind. Coal can be difficult to light. Coal also takes up a lot of space, so it is difficult to store.

c **What is the advantage of having a coal fire if there is an electricity power cut?**

The main user of coal today is the electricity supply industry. Coal is their most common source of energy.

Natural gas

Natural gas is the gas we use at home to cook with and to heat our central heating boiler. Its chemical name is methane.

If there is not enough oxygen when the methane is burned, carbon monoxide is formed.

Carbon monoxide is very poisonous and can kill very quickly. About thirty people die from carbon monoxide poisoning every year in this country. This often happens when gas water heaters or central heating boilers have not been serviced properly.

d **Carbon monoxide is found in coal mines. Suggest why miners used to take canaries down mines with them before carbon monoxide detectors were made.**

TASKS

1 A house owner needs to replace his central heating boiler. He can choose between oil, coal and natural gas as the fuel.
   a Other than cost, what are the advantages and disadvantages of using each fuel?
   b The house owner needs to know how much it will cost him to heat his home every year. Suggest where he could find the information he needs.
   c Now find the information for yourself. How much does it cost to heat an average-sized home for a year using each fuel?

More questions CD-ROM

5.2 Problems with fossil fuels

You may have heard about the **greenhouse effect** and **acid rain**. Both of these problems are caused by burning fossil fuels.

The greenhouse effect

You know that carbon dioxide is produced when all fossil fuels burn.

Carbon dioxide in the atmosphere acts like the glass in a greenhouse. Carbon dioxide is known as a '**greenhouse gas**'. It allows energy from the Sun to pass through but then traps it. The trapped energy warms the atmosphere.

More and more carbon dioxide is being produced by industry. This has led to rising sea levels as a result of the polar ice caps melting. Sea levels could rise by as much as 1 m by the year 2100.

Over the past 100 years, the average sea level has risen by 10 to 15 cm. If the problem continues to get worse, many low lying parts of the world will be flooded. These include cities like New York and London.

a What may happen to the polar ice caps in the next hundred years?

b What will happen to sea levels as a result?

Acid rain

When some fossil fuels are burned, a gas called sulfur dioxide is produced. This gas dissolves in rainwater to form acid rain.

Acid rain burns the leaves on living trees. These trees in Port Talbot, South Wales, have been killed by the pollution from factories and power stations which burn fossil fuels. The trees were just 30 years old.

c Trees convert carbon dioxide to oxygen during photosynthesis. What difference would there be in the greenhouse effect if a lot of the world's trees were damaged by acid rain?

Non-renewable

The other major problem with fossil fuels is that they are being used up. They are **non-renewable energy** sources.

Coal, oil and gas have taken millions of years to form, but most of the **reserves** (the amounts we know exist) have been used during the past few hundred years.

TASKS

1 This table shows the known amounts (reserves) of coal and oil in some parts of the world and how much was produced in 2001. Reserves/production shows how long the fuel will last if it continues to be extracted at the present rate.

	North America	South/ Central America	Europe	Former Soviet Union	Middle East/ Africa	Asia/ Pacific	United Kingdom	World
COAL								
Reserves, in millions of tonnes	258 000	22 000	125 000	230 000	57 000	292 000	1500	984 000
Production in 2001, in millions of tonnes	1100	60	750	440	230	1990	30	4570
Reserves/production, in years	235	367	167	523	248	147	50	215
OIL								
Reserves, in millions of tonnes	8400	13 700	2500	9000	103 600	5900	700	143 100
Production in 2001, in millions of tonnes	660	350	320	420	1450	380	120	3580
Reserves/production, in years	13	39	8	21	71	16	6	40

a If the United Kingdom did not import coal, when would we run out of coal?
b Which part of the world has most coal reserves?
c Which part of the world has most oil reserves?
d Explain why parts of the world with large reserves of coal may run out before parts of the world with less coal.

Nuclear power stations produce nearly one-fifth of the world's total supply of electricity. The one in the photograph is at Hinkley Point in Somerset.

In some countries more than half of the electricity produced comes from nuclear power stations.

All power stations produce electricity, but they also produce things we don't want.

Coal-fired stations produce ash. They also produce gases that are harmful to the environment. These gases include carbon dioxide, sulphur dioxide and nitrogen oxides.

The good thing about nuclear power stations is that they do not produce these gases. If the electricity produced from nuclear power came from fossil fuels instead, an extra 1600 million tonnes of carbon dioxide would be produced each year.

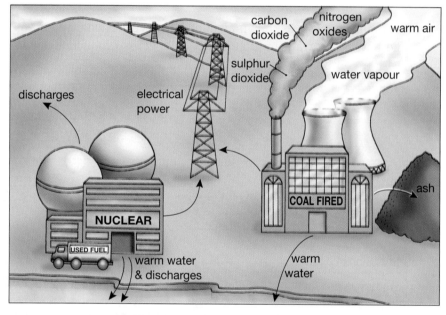

a Why is it good to cut down on the amounts of carbon dioxide produced?

b Why is it good to cut down on the amounts of sulphur dioxide produced?

A nuclear power station uses uranium or plutonium as a fuel instead of burning fossil fuels. Uranium and plutonium are both elements. They are also **radioactive**. This means they give off radiation.

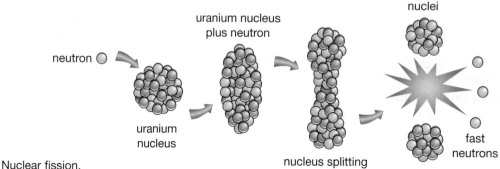

Nuclear fission.

In the power station, the uranium or plutonium is split. This produces huge amounts of energy as heat, used to make electricity in the way seen in fossil fuel power stations.

Concerns with nuclear power

Many people are opposed to an increased use of nuclear power. They want to see fewer nuclear power stations. In April 1986, there was an explosion at Chernobyl, a nuclear power station in the Ukraine. Forty people died as a result. Some of the radioactive material from the power station was released into the atmosphere and blown by the wind across Russia and Europe. Some Welsh farmers still could not sell their lambs five years later because the grass had been **contaminated**.

Another major concern is the radioactive waste that nuclear power stations produce. There are problems storing the waste, getting rid of the waste or **reprocessing** the waste to make new fuel.

Nuclear power stations produce three levels of waste. These are known as low level, intermediate level and high level.

- Most of the waste is low level waste. Some liquid waste is safely piped into the sea and some solid waste is burned. The rest is sorted, compressed and stored in containers at a special waste site.
- Most intermediate level waste comes from nuclear power stations. It is broken down, mixed with concrete and stored in very large steel drums. The drums are then stored inside the power station or at a nuclear reprocessing plant.
- High level waste is the most dangerous and can remain radioactive for a very long time – maybe thousands of years. This waste is very hot and is stored as a liquid in water-cooled tanks before it is mixed with glass, and finally stored in steel drums in a cooled vault behind thick concrete. It is very expensive to store nuclear waste safely and this is a big disadvantage.

c Why are the vaults for storing high level waste made of thick concrete?

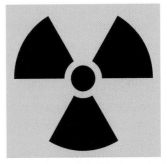

'Danger – radioactivity' symbol

A drum of intermediate level waste.

A storage area for intermediate level waste.

TASKS

1 Most nuclear power stations are built near the coast and away from populated areas.
   a On an outline map of the United Kingdom, plot the location of each nuclear power station.
   b On the same map, plot the location of the town nearest to each power station.
   c Draw up a list of arguments for and against the use of nuclear power. Suggest which of these may have been used in deciding the locations of the nuclear power stations.

More questions

You will have seen in the newspapers or in television news programmes that people protest about the building of such things as housing estates, factories or power stations near to their homes. In Wales, they are protesting about windmills!

In June 2002, newspapers reported that a protest campaign had begun to stop a **wind farm** from being built.

YMGYRCH
CEFN CROES
CAMPAIGN

Welsh Planners Get Wind of Protest

THE government plans to use more wind farms to produce electricity for the nation. A spokesperson for the Department of Energy said 'Wind farms are a clean solution to our energy problems'. But protestors are angry that local planners have given the go-ahead to build the largest British wind farm in the mountains of Mid-Wales.

Thirty-nine **wind turbines** would fill the whole length of the distant mountain ridge shown in the photograph. There are plans for another 165 turbines to be built 10 miles away.

a Why are the tops of mountains chosen for wind farms?

How windfarms work

Britain is the windiest country in Europe. The energy from the wind could produce three times the electricity needs of the country.

Wind turbines turn as the wind blows to produce electricity. Some turbines, including those proposed for mid-Wales, are over 100 metres tall. That is more than twice the height of Nelson's Column.

Some small wind turbines are used on their own to power small machines or charge batteries. Often, 20 or more large turbines are grouped together to make a wind farm. A farm like this would take up a site of about 4 km² but only 1% of that area is taken up by the actual machines. The rest can be farmed normally.

Would you want a wind turbine twice as big as this column near your house?

Different perspectives

Wind turbines are designed to last between 15 and 25 years. After that, they can be dismantled without producing any dangerous waste products.

Wind farms do not produce the same pollution as fossil fuel power stations. A power station burning a fossil fuel and producing the same amount of electricity as the wind farm proposed for mid-Wales would produce at least 150 000 tonnes of carbon dioxide every year. Carbon dioxide is a greenhouse gas.

b What is meant by the term 'greenhouse gas'?

Some people object to the sight of wind turbines and others object to the noise of the rotors. At the moment, nearly half of all wind turbines are in Wales. The Government also wants wind farms to be built at least 3 miles offshore.

While the people of Wales are protesting, the Scottish Friends of the Earth are more welcoming of proposals for wind power in Scotland. 'This proposal has many significant attractions. It will harness Scotland's wind resource, which is the best in Europe; it will displace fossil fuel demand and help us meet our international obligations to tackle climate change.'

TASKS

1 You are a resident living near the site of a proposed wind farm.
   a Write a letter to your local MP explaining your objections to the wind farm.
   b Write a reply from the Department for Energy, answering the objections in your letter.

2 Write a letter to your local MP or to a local newspaper in support of the proposed wind farm.

There are other **renewable energy** sources that are providing us with energy.

Solar power

Solar cells use light from the Sun to produce electricity.

- They can be used in this country to power small electrical devices such as calculators.
- In countries nearer the equator they are able to produce more electricity.

a Why are solar cells more useful in India than they are in the UK?

In space, solar cells are used to provide all of the electricity needs of spacecraft. The electricity produced is used to power the spacecraft and to charge up batteries.

b Why does the spacecraft need to use batteries instead of just solar cells?

The energy from the Sun can also be used to heat water in **solar panels**. Even in this country, it is possible to save money on water heating bills.

c Why must solar panels in this country be mounted on south-facing roofs but in Australia be mounted on north-facing roofs?

Hydroelectric power

Another common energy source is water. In mountain regions, the energy from falling water is used to turn turbines. These turn generators, which produce electricity.
A power station like this can be operating at full power just 10 seconds after the water starts to flow from the reservoir. This means that a sudden demand for electricity can be met without any problem.

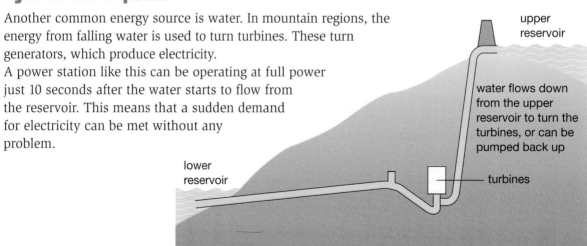

upper reservoir

water flows down from the upper reservoir to turn the turbines, or can be pumped back up

lower reservoir

turbines

d Suggest why there is often a sudden demand for electricity at the end of a film on television.

Most **hydroelectric power stations** have only one reservoir, with the water continuing to flow along a river. The reservoirs are often made larger with a dam.

Some hydroelectric power stations pump water back from a lower reservoir to an upper reservoir during the night.

e Why is the water pumped back during the night?

There are not many places where there are two natural reservoirs for a hydroelectric power station to be built. This means that a valley has to be flooded.

If the energy produced by hydroelectric power stations was produced by fossil fuels instead, an extra two billion tonnes of carbon dioxide would be produced every year.

The River Severn is a suitable place to build a **tidal barrage** hydroelectric power station. This is a long barrage across the mouth of a river.

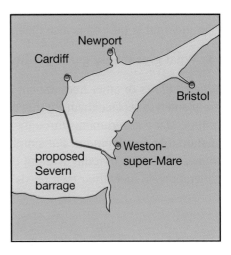

- As the tide comes in, the water passes through tubes in the barrage and turns turbines to produce electricity.
- When the tide goes out, the turbines work in reverse to produce more electricity.

A power station across the mouth of the Rance estuary in Brittany, France, has been producing electricity since 1966.

Other forms of renewable energy include wave power. The up and down motion of the waves turns a turbine to produce electricity.

TASKS

1 The building of a hydroelectric power station could mean that valleys become flooded, and a tidal barrage could affect mudflats and beaches near the estuary.

Are the benefits of hydroelectric power greater than any environmental problems which may be caused?

Biofuel

These two cars look very similar. They are both Subaru Imprezas.

One car uses petrol obtained from crude oil, a fossil fuel.

The other car uses fuel obtained from sugar.

As we have already seen, fossil fuels are running out, and we need alternative sources of energy.

Sugar is obtained from a plant, and when the plant is harvested another plant can be grown. The sugar is fermented and distilled to produce bioethanol. This is one example of a **biofuel**. Most cars can use a mixture of 10% bioethanol and 90% petrol without modifying the engine. Some cars can run on fuel with up to 85% bioethanol.

Biomass is all of the plant and animal matter on the Earth's surface. The energy contained within the biomass is called **bioenergy**. A biofuel is biomass that is burned to release the energy.

Some people think that any form of burning is bad for the environment because of the greenhouse gases which are produced. The fuel that is burned is also destroyed.

a What greenhouse gas is produced when a fuel burns?

When willows or other trees are cut down to be burned, other trees are planted to replace them. In this way, there is a continuing supply of fuel. Many governments throughout the world are encouraging **sustainable development**. Put simply, this is 'the ability of mankind to meet the needs of today without compromising the ability of future generations to meet their own needs'.

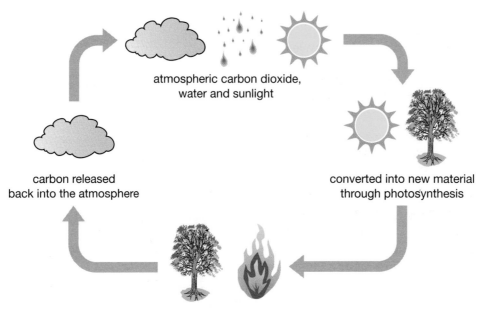

atmospheric carbon dioxide, water and sunlight

carbon released back into the atmosphere

converted into new material through photosynthesis

which is harvested and burnt

The carbon dioxide produced when the wood burns is absorbed by the newly planted trees. The trees convert the carbon dioxide to energy by photosynthesis.

Trees are planted and allowed to grow at the rate at which they are cut down for burning. Therefore the carbon dioxide released when the wood is burned is never more than the carbon dioxide absorbed by new trees.

b Explain why the use of biofuels is said to be 'CO_2 neutral'.

Bioethanol and biodiesel

Both bioethanol and biodiesel are cleaner fuels than their fossil fuel counterparts. They release up to 60% less carbon dioxide when burned. Combustion of a blend of 10% bioethanol and 90% petrol will release 6% less carbon dioxide than that produced by using pure petrol.

c Jeremy has modified his car to run on a mixture of 25% bioethanol and 75% petrol. Up to what percentage reduction in carbon dioxide emission can he expect?

Biodiesel is produced from palm oil or rapeseed. Unfortunately, the cost of producing biodiesel straight from agricultural sources makes it uneconomical at the present time. But if the cost of diesel goes up or the technology becomes cheaper, we may find our lorries and buses using biodiesel as their fuel.

There is a possibility that cooking oil can be used as a biofuel. In some areas of the country, waste cooking oil from restaurants is collected regularly and converted into biodiesel.

Nuclear fusion

You have already seen how nuclear fission, the splitting of nuclei, is used in power stations to produce energy. Energy is also released when the nuclei of two light atoms, such as isotopes of hydrogen, are forced to join together. This is called **nuclear fusion** and is the process by which the Sun produces its energy.

Scientists have made nuclear fusion happen in the laboratory. They are trying to make it work on a larger scale. This might be another way to help supply the energy we need.

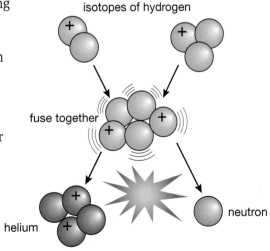

5.7 Energy transfer

Whenever you work on your computer, watch television or listen to your CD player, energy is being transferred.

If you feel your computer after it has been switched on for a while, it is warm.

a Why do larger PCs have fans in them?

b The casing of a PC has a grill by the fan to allow heat to escape. Why is it important not to cover this grill?

The television you watch gets warm. Your CD player gets warm, too. Anything with a motor inside gets warm.

It does not matter what energy transfer is happening, some energy always ends up heating the surroundings. When energy is spread out in the surroundings in this way it is no longer useful. The energy is not lost; it is just in a form which is not useful.

As you boil the water, energy is lost to the air, the water and the saucepan.

Inside a car engine

A car engine is designed to transfer the energy stored in the fuel into **kinetic** (movement) **energy**, but a lot of heat is also produced. As the pistons move up and down, **friction** produces heat.

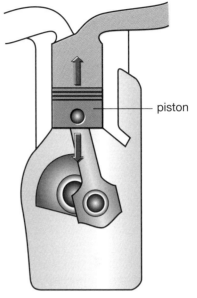

piston

The piston moves up and down.

c Heat is produced in the engine. How is it removed?

d Why is oil put into an engine?

e The original Volkswagen Beetle was designed with its engine at the back of the car. It does not have a radiator. The engine cover has slits in it. How does the engine keep cool?

TASKS

1 Choose another energy transfer device which produces a lot of energy that heats up the surroundings.
   a How is the heat produced in this device?
   b How is the device designed to keep cool?

More questions   CD-ROM

5.8 Generating electricity

Most of the electricity used in the United Kingdom comes from burning fossil fuels in a power station.

The process in a coal power station

1 Coal for the power station arrives by train.

a Suggest why the coal arrives by train and not by road.

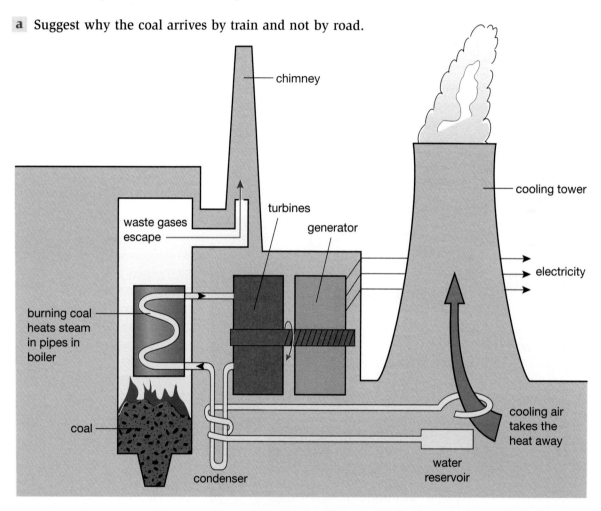

2 The coal is crushed before being burned in the furnace. This makes it burn better.

b When coal burns, ash is produced. Suggest how it is removed from the power station and disposed of.

3 Water in the boiler is heated and turns to steam. By heating the water under pressure, the boiling point of the water is raised to 700°C.

c What is the normal boiling point of water?

d Suggest what problems there are with heating water to 700°C under pressure.

4 The steam turns a **turbine** which is connected to a **generator**.

5 The generator produces electricity.

6 The steam is **condensed** back to water as it passes through cooling towers. What you see coming from the top of the cooling towers is water vapour, not smoke as many people think. The waste gases come out of the tall chimneys.

7 The water returns to the boiler.

This is a very inefficient way to generate electricity. The table shows the energy losses through the power station.

Place where energy is wasted	Percentage wasted
boiler	15
cooling tower	45
generator	5

e The rest of the energy is useful electricity. What percentage of the input energy is turned into useful output?

Using electricity

Most of us use electricity every day – in houses, offices, farms and factories. It is convenient because it is easy to use and can operate a wide variety of appliances. There is no pollution at the point we use it and there are no storage problems.

But there are disadvantages to using electricity. Cables are needed to bring it to our homes, and because it cannot be stored there are risks of power cuts. If there is any fault, we can receive an electric shock.

TASKS

1 Most of the energy wasted from a power station goes into the atmosphere from the cooling towers.
   What could be done with the hot water produced in the cooling towers?

2 Draw a pie-chart to show where the energy in a power station is used and wasted.

3 Power stations used to be built inland near coal mines. Nowadays, a lot of coal is imported from other countries. Where would you suggest building a coal-fired power station today?

More questions

5.9 The right fuel for the job

A **fuel** is a chemical which burns to release energy as heat.

There are many fuels and they each have properties which make them useful in a particular situation. There is no such thing as the best fuel. The fuel that is best for the job depends on each particular situation.

How to decide

These are some of the questions we need to ask when choosing a fuel for a particular situation.

- How easy is it to light?
- How long does it burn for when lit?
- How hot is the flame?
- Does it produce ash or smoke?
- How easy is it to store or transport?
- How much does it cost?

Examples of decisions

You may live in a house in the country, miles from anywhere. The house may not have a chimney. You heat your living room with a mobile gas heater. The heater contains a gas cylinder.

a Suggest why this is a good choice of fuel to heat the room.

b Suggest another situation where gas cylinders are often used.

Any gas cylinder can be very dangerous if it is put into a fire. The pressure of the gas builds up until the cylinder explodes. The gas is suddenly released into the surroundings and catches fire.

In school science lessons, students heat chemicals with Bunsen burners. These too work from a gas supply. In towns and most villages this comes from a mains gas supply, but in some rural areas where there is no mains gas the supply is from cylinders.

c Suggest why mains gas is preferred instead of cylinders for Bunsen burners.

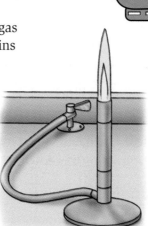

Most road and rail transport relies on oil-based products such as petrol, diesel or kerosene.

- Quad bikes use petrol, which needs a spark to make the vapour ignite in the engine.
- Buses, lorries and some train engines use diesel as a fuel.
- Aircraft use kerosene.

d What property does petrol have which makes it a good fuel for quad bike engines?

e What other vehicles use petrol as a fuel?

TASKS

1 Most people use petrol to run their cars. However, more cars are using diesel and a significant number are now using liquefied petroleum gas (LPG), sometimes called Autogas.

Premium litre	87.9
Autogas litre	42.9
LRP litre	93.9
Diesel litre	88.9
Shop	JET WASH

Try to find out all you can about diesel fuel and LPG.

a How is a car using diesel or a car using LPG different from one using petrol?
b What are the advantages and disadvantages of using diesel?
c What are the advantages and disadvantages of using LPG?

Your local garage is planning to convert cars to run on LPG instead of petrol. This means fitting a tank into the boot of the car.

d Write an advertising leaflet for the garage to give out to people who might be thinking of changing their cars to run on LPG.

More questions CD-ROM

The term 'energy **efficiency**' is used in two slightly different ways. In the home and at work, we use the term to mean making the best use of the energy available and wasting as little as possible.

Home, warm home

Everyone enjoys sitting round a traditional coal or log fire during those long winter evenings, but this is not the best way of heating the room.

a Where does most of the heat energy from an open fire go?

An open fire burning in the hearth radiates energy into the room. For every 100 units of energy produced as heat by the burning fuel, between 20 and 30 units radiate into the room.

b What percentage of the energy produced by an open fire is used to heat the room?

c What percentage of the energy produced by an open fire is wasted?

We say that an open fire is not very efficient because so much of the energy is wasted.

A modern room heater burning logs or coal can radiate up to 50 units of energy into the room.

d Why does this type of coal fire radiate more heat into the room?

e What percentage of the energy produced by a modern room heater is used to heat the room?

f What percentage of the energy produced by a modern room heater is wasted?

In both fires, the same proportion of energy stored in the coal is transferred as heat by the burning coal. It is the design of the fire which has made the modern room heater more efficient.

Calculating efficiency

Scientists measure energy efficiency when energy is transferred.

$$\text{energy efficiency} = \frac{\text{useful energy output}}{\text{total energy input}}$$

When Cathy runs, she exerts a force of 75 N for a distance of 400 m.

We use this equation to find her useful energy output in joules.

$$\text{energy} = \text{force} \times \text{distance moved}$$

g What is Cathy's useful energy output?

As we saw in Chapter 2, Cathy gets her energy from the food she eats. While running, Cathy uses up 150 000 joules of food energy.

h What is Cathy's energy efficiency?

Sometimes, energy efficiency is quoted as a percentage.

$$\text{percentage energy efficiency} = \frac{\text{useful energy output}}{\text{total energy input}} \times 100\%$$

i What is Cathy's percentage efficiency?

The energy which Cathy does not transfer into movement is transferred into heat. This is why athletes get very hot and sweaty.

Car manufacturers are trying to improve the fuel economy (miles per gallon) of cars. This marks cars more efficient and reduces their running costs.

TASKS

1 The modern room heater is more efficient than the old-fashioned fire.
   a How does this affect the amount of coal burned?
   b How does this affect the fuel costs of the home?
   c Explain how other forms of heating could be even more efficient.

2 **Multigym**
   Portfolio Unit 1, Unit 3 CD-ROM

 **More questions** CD-ROM

5.11 Filament light bulbs

It can be very hot to be on stage under powerful stage lights.

The bulbs in the stage lights are **filament** light bulbs. Inside they have a thin metal wire called a filament. This becomes hot and glows when an electric current passes through it.

a Why does a filament light bulb have to get hot?

When a filament light bulb is used, much of the energy is lost as heat. It is not turned to light. This heats up both the bulb and air around it.

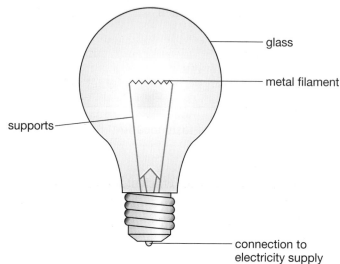

glass

metal filament

supports

connection to electricity supply

b Why is it so hot under stage lights?

Representing energy transfers

The diagram shows the energy from the electricity supply and the heat and light it makes. The width of the arrows shows the energy transferred as heat and light.

100 units of energy supplied to the bulb

95 units of energy used to heat the bulb and the air

c How many units of energy are transferred as light?

The filament bulb is very inefficient as a source of light. This is because it transfers so little of the electrical energy as light.

TASKS

1 a Make a list of the power rating in watts of all filament bulbs in your home.
  b Choose one bulb and keep a record of how long it is switched on in one week. You may need to design a record card to place near the switch for everyone at home to log the use of the bulb.
  c The table shows the electrical energy supplied to different bulbs in one hour.

Power rating of bulb in watts	Energy used by the bulb in 1 hour in kW
40	0.04
60	0.06
100	0.10

  d Work out the energy supplied to your bulb in kilowatt-hours in one year (52 weeks).
  e 1 kilowatt-hour of electricity costs 7p. What does it cost to use the bulb for a year?
  f How much of that money is used to heat the bulb and the air around it?
    You can work it out like this:

$$\text{Cost of heating bulb and air} = \text{cost of using bulb} \times \tfrac{95}{100}$$

Portfolio Unit 3 c1, d1

5.12 Energy-saving light bulbs

You may have seen light bulbs which look quite different from filament bulbs.

People today want to save energy. One way of saving energy, and money, is to use bulbs which turn more energy to light than a filament light bulb.

An energy-saving light bulb, like the one on the right, works in a different way from a filament bulb. It has a gas inside it which gives off **ultraviolet radiation** when an electric current passes through it.

The ultraviolet radiation is turned into light we can see by a chemical on the inside of the bulb. The diagram shows how the energy of one of these bulbs is turned into heat and light.

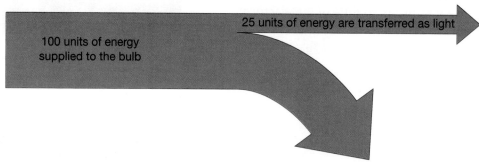

25 units of energy are transferred as light

100 units of energy supplied to the bulb

a How many units of energy are wasted as heat from the 100 units of energy supplied to an energy-saving light bulb?

This is still a lot of energy wasted, but much less than is wasted from a filament light bulb. If every home in the United Kingdom used just one energy-saving light bulb, the energy saved would be the same as the energy produced by a nuclear power station.

Comparing light bulbs

Energy-saving bulbs use less electrical energy to produce the same amount of light as a filament light bulb. A 20 W energy-saving light bulb produces the same amount of light as a 100 W filament light bulb! Energy-saving light bulbs also last longer, especially if used in places where lights stay on for a long time.

Energy-saving light bulbs do have some drawbacks. They are more expensive to buy than filament light bulbs. They also take some time to warm up. When you first switch them on they are very dim – this is a bit annoying if you want instant light.

The table shows the costs of buying and using two bulbs that provide the same amount of light.

Assume that electricity costs 7p per kilowatt hour.

Type of bulb	Cost of bulb	Lifetime, in hours	Power rating, in watts	Electrical cost for 15 000 hours use
filament	£0.25	1500	100	£105.00
energy-saving	£6.00	15 000	20	£21.00

b What is the total cost of lighting a room with a 20 W energy-saving light bulb for 15 000 hours?

c What is the total cost of lighting a room with a 100 W filament light bulb for 15 000 hours?

d How much money is saved by using the energy-saving bulb?

TASKS

1 The manager of the Grand Hotel has to replace the lighting in the main entrance hall, the corridors and the bedrooms.

The Grand Hotel has 500 bedrooms, each of which has seven bulbs. There are 1000 bulbs in the main entrance hall and corridors. The bulbs in the entrance hall and corridors have to be on all the time.

Suggest where the hotel manager should consider using energy-saving light bulbs and where she should continue to use filament light bulbs. Explain in detail the reasons for your suggestions.

You will have heard adults complaining when the gas and electricity bills arrive. They often complain about the amount of energy wasted around the home: doors are left open, lights, computers and CD players are left switched on …

Usable energy is limited, expensive and we all need to do as much as we can to save it.

The people who live in this house can do a lot to help. Even drawing the curtains in the attic room will help.

The picture (a **thermogram**) has been taken with a special camera which shows temperature instead of light. The colour coding ranges from white to yellow for the warmest areas through red to purple and green for the coolest areas. Thermograms are often used to check houses for heat loss. The house can then be made more energy efficient through improved **insulation**.

a Which parts of the house are losing most heat?

A house with no insulation loses most heat through the walls.

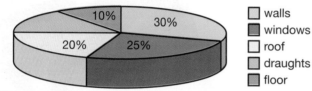

- walls
- windows
- roof
- draughts
- floor

b What percentage of heat loss is through draughts?

Heat is lost from a house by **conduction**, **convection** and **radiation**. The energy is transferred from a region of high temperature to a region of lower temperature.

Cavity wall insulation

Modern houses are built with a gap between the outer and inner walls. This gap contains air.

Air is a very poor conductor of heat, so it reduces heat loss by conduction. But air is a very good convector, so warm air will rise through the cavity into the loft.

Cavity wall insulation is made of a material which has a lot of trapped air in it. However, the air cannot move so heat loss by convection is reduced as well.

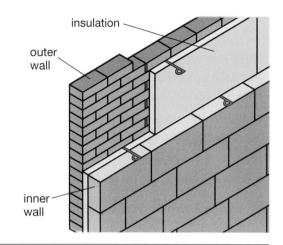

Loft insulation

Fibreglass or mineral wool is placed between the timber joists across the floor of the loft. Again air is trapped in the material and reduces heat loss by conduction and convection.

Double glazing

Air is trapped between two layers of glass and reduces the amount of heat lost by conduction.

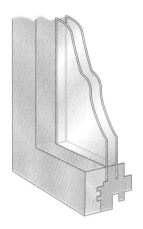

Reflecting heat

Energy from radiators on the wall passes into the room but also passes from the back of the radiator through the wall. Shiny foil on the wall behind the radiator reflects the energy back into the room and reduces heat loss by radiation.

To help people reduce energy losses, local councils advise and give grants for energy saving.

TASKS

1 A house owner decides to insulate his house.
   a Find out how much it costs to install loft insulation, cavity wall insulation and double glazing.
   b Which energy saving option will save the house owner the most money in the future?

When the three little pigs built their houses, there wasn't the choice of materials we have today.

You learned about clay bricks in Chapter 4. The brick house was certainly the strongest, but today people who design buildings have to think about other factors. One such factor is energy efficiency.

Straw buildings are now becoming more common in this country, although in America they have been using straw for a number of years.

In Belfast, some children study in a straw classroom.

a Explain why straw is a good material to use for the walls of a house.

Timber houses too are becoming far more common. Many houses that have brick exteriors have timber frames inside.

A Devon health centre has been built around an old kiln. The walls of the building have a dense, concrete inner skin, with 200 mm of insulation on the outside. The outer wall is timber. The concrete acts like a night storage heater, absorbing and storing the heat to release when it is cooler.

The heating effect is so good that during the first winter, the central heating was not turned on until December. The energy saving during the 20-year life of the building is estimated to be at least £150 000.

Saving energy by design

People who design buildings today think about all aspects of energy saving.

Two common materials used to make window frames are aluminium and wood.

	Aluminium	Wood
energy needed to produce window frame	100 energy units	1 energy unit
heat transfer	good conductor	poor conductor
weight	very light	heavy

b What other material is often used to make window frames?

c Suggest one advantage of using aluminium window frames and one advantage of using wooden window frames.

Recycled, shredded paper is often used as loft insulation material.

Energy-efficient buildings should use:

- local materials wherever possible
- materials which do not use a lot of energy to produce
- timber
- materials with low **thermal conductivity** (this is a measure of how well a material conducts heat)
- materials without hazardous side-effects.

d The thermal conductivity of fibreglass is 0.04 units, of rubber is 0.15 units and of polystyrene is 0.08 units. Which is the best material to put in the loft as insulation?

TASKS

1 You have been asked to choose materials for a new building for your school. You can decide what the building is to be used for.
   a Choose the building materials you would use – you do not have to use the ones in this list.
   b Think about the other factors to consider.
   c Explain the reasons for your choices.

Thermal conductivities of common building materials

Walls		Roof	
Brickwork (outer leaf)	0.77	Asphalt	0.70
Brickwork (inner leaf)	0.56	Concrete slab	0.16
Lightweight aggregate concrete block	0.57	Felt/bitumen layers	0.23
Autoclaved aerated concrete block	0.18	Screed	0.41
Concrete	1.59	Stone chippings	2.0
Reinforced concrete	2.4	Tiles (clay)	1.0
Mortar	0.91	Tiles (concrete)	1.5
Sandstone	2.3	**Floor**	
Limestone	1.4	Cast concrete	1.35
Fibreboard	0.1	Steel	50.0
Plasterboard	0.25	Screed	0.41
Ceramic tiles	1.3	Timber	0.16
Timber	0.16	**Insulation**	
Surface finish		Expanded polystyrene	0.040
External rendering	0.57	Mineral wool	0.040
Plaster	0.57	Polyurethane	0.025

2 Aircraft construction
   Portfolio Unit 1

It would save a lot of energy if the waste heat we produce could be reused.

A **heat exchanger** is a device that captures and recycles energy. It uses the heat from one process to provide the heat for another.

At home

Not everyone has a swimming pool in their garden. In the United Kingdom the pool would get very cold in winter.

This pool uses the heat from the domestic central heating system to heat the pool water.

Water from the domestic hot water system is pumped through the heat exchanger. It surrounds the water which is being pumped from the swimming pool.

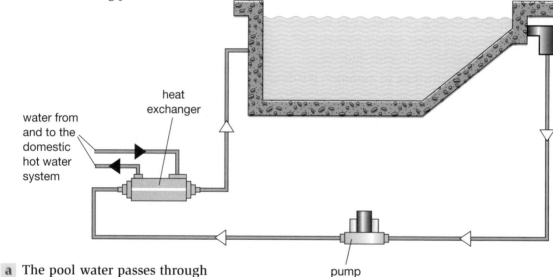

a The pool water passes through a large number of small tubes instead of one large tube. Suggest why.

It is not only swimming pools for humans that use heat exchangers. Koi and other tropical fish need to be kept in warm pools if they are to survive.

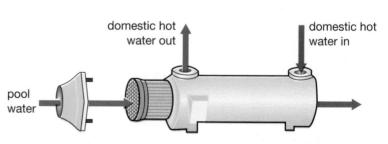

In the home, and in industry, refrigerators use a heat exchanger to remove heat. In the freezing compartment, a volatile liquid evaporates, removing heat from the freezer. The vapour is pumped into the heat exchanger (the pipes with cooling fins at the back of the refrigerator). Here it is compressed, changes back to a liquid and gives out heat to the surrounding air.

On the road

Although most car engines are cooled by water, some are cooled by the air.

This Porsche has a heat exchanger which uses the heat from the engine to provide heat for the inside of the car when it is cold.

The modern Porsche has a water-cooled engine, but still uses a heat exchanger to transfer the waste heat from the engine oil to the coolant. Heat is discharged via radiators.

Water is used as the coolant in radiators because it has a very high **specific heat capacity**. This means that water can absorb a lot of heat without a large rise in temperature. Even so, the temperature of the water in the cooling system of a modern car can go above 135°C.

At the other extreme, in winter when the car is standing out in the road, the temperature can be well below freezing.

b What are the normal boiling and freezing points of water?

When any impurity is added to water, it raises the boiling point and lowers the freezing point. This is why we put salt on the roads in winter.

Antifreeze is an impurity added to the cooling system of a car to make sure that the water in the cooling system stays liquid at temperatures below the normal freezing point.

H More on heat exchangers CD-ROM

TASKS

1 The makers of antifreeze recommend that 1 litre of antifreeze is added to 3 litres of water.
Investigate what happens to the freezing point of water if more or less antifreeze is added. Note that antifreeze contains ethylene glycol, which is a poison.

Energy is money

Every electrical appliance costs money to run. Even the latest games console or mini system adds a few pence to your electricity bill every time it is used.

Every electrical appliance has a **power rating**. This is a measure of how quickly energy from the electrical supply is transferred. The larger the power rating, the quicker energy is being transferred.

power = voltage × current

Most electrical appliances have a label on them which looks something like this.

MODEL S244			
SERIAL No 11235426			
230–250 V	5 A	~50 Hz	1.2 kW
Made in UK			

This tells you that the appliance is to be used with a mains supply with a voltage of between 230 and 250 volts. In the UK the mains voltage is 230 V. The power of the appliance is 1.2 kilowatts (kW), or 1200 watts (W).

$$\text{power (in W)} = \frac{\text{energy (in J)}}{\text{time (in s)}}$$

A toaster has a power rating of 1200 W. This means it transfers 1200 joules of energy each second.

A desk lamp has a much lower power rating. It is only 60 W.

a How many joules of energy does the desk lamp transfer each second?

When does a toaster stop 'toasting' a slice of bread?

Longer use means bigger bills

The energy transferred in the home is not measured in joules. It is measured in **kilowatt-hours**.

If a 1 kW appliance, such as a single bar of an electric fire, is switched on for 1 hour, it transfers 1 kilowatt-hour (kWh) of energy.

energy transferred (in kWh) = power rating (in kW) × time (in h)

b How much energy is transferred by a 3 kW immersion heater in 30 minutes (half an hour)?

cost of electricity = energy transferred (in kWh) × cost per kWh (in pence)

c If electricity costs 7p per kWh, how much does it cost when the 3 kW immersion heater is switched on for 30 minutes?

The energy transfer is measured by your electricity meter. You will find your electricity meter either near the consumer unit which contains the fuses and switches or in an outside cupboard.

When you read the meter, you ignore the last number.
The reading on this meter is 19919.

The company which supplies electricity to your home usually receives a meter reading every three months and calculates the total energy transferred.

d The reading on the meter shown above three months later is 20779. How many kWh of energy have been transferred?

TASKS

1 Find the electricity meter in your home.
   Find out how much you pay for each kWh of electricity.
   a Read the meter at the same time every day for a week.
   b What day shows the biggest increase? Suggest why.
   c How much does the electricity in your home cost each day for the week?

It is unlikely that your electricity bill at home will be this big, but schools, offices and factories spend thousands of pounds a month on electricity.

In the United Kingdom, there are over a thousand different ways in which electricity is charged.

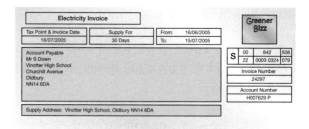

One example

This school buys its electricity from a company which invests in renewable energy.

The supply company makes sure that there is 200 kW available for the school to use.

It is cheaper to use electricity at night. More is used during the day.

This is a fixed charge for supplying the electricity. It does not depend on how much is used.

The supply company invests this money in buying electricity from renewable energy sources.

The government takes a proportion of the charges as VAT.

Account details
Period of Supply 16/06/2005 to 15/07/2005

	Rate/Basis of Charge	Units	Amount £
Contract Charges			
Availability Charge	£1.02 / kW	200 kW	204.00
Consumption Day Rate	3.63p / kWh	19206 kWh	697.18
Consumption Night Rate	2.45p / kWh	2956 kWh	72.42
Standing Charge			17.40
Contract Charges Sub Total			**991.00**
Levies			
Renewable Energy Benefit	0.43p / kWh	22162 kWh	95.30
Levies Sub Total			**95.30**
Sales Tax Charges			
VAT @ 5%	5%		54.32
Sales Tax Charges Sub Total			**54.32**
Total Amount Payable			**1140.62**

a How many kWh of electricity did the school use in the month?

b Suggest why the school might have decided to pay extra for renewable energy.

c Why is electricity less expensive during the night?

Choices

Some supply companies make a fixed charge to pay for the upkeep of the cables and transmission lines that supply the electricity. These charges have to be made no matter how much electricity is used. This means the charge is the same for every customer. Other companies charge more for the electricity supplied instead.

TASKS

1 Read the following extracts from three different supply companies.

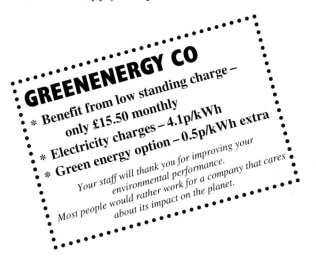

GREENENERGY CO
* Benefit from low standing charge – only £15.50 monthly
* Electricity charges – 4.1p/kWh
* Green energy option – 0.5p/kWh extra

Your staff will thank you for improving your environmental performance.
Most people would rather work for a company that cares about its impact on the planet.

MEGWATT LTD
No standing charge
Monthly billing
All electricity charged at 4.9p/kWh

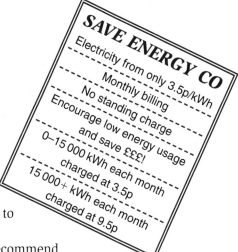

SAVE ENERGY CO
Electricity from only 3.5p/kWh
Monthly billing
No standing charge
Encourage low energy usage and save £££!
0–15 000 kWh each month charged at 3.5p
15 000+ kWh each month charged at 9.5p

A school uses up to 25 000 kWh each month.
a Use the information provided by each company to produce graphs comparing the monthly costs.
b Which electricity supply company would you recommend the school uses? Explain the reasons for your choice.

You will have seen science fiction films or watched the battles between robots on television.

The robots of science fiction are now becoming everyday examples of science fact.

Robots are taking over some of the boring, repetitive jobs on factory assembly lines.

a What are the advantages of using robots instead of humans on a factory assembly line?

Scientists at the Transport Research Laboratory use crash test dummies to **model** (monitor) how humans might react in crash situations.

b What are the advantages of using dummies instead of humans in crash tests?

Surgery

- Sometimes when operating, doctors have to use a robot.
- Humans cannot make a hole exactly one $\frac{1}{4}$ mm wide and long, but robots can.
- Robots make medicines much faster and more accurately (with better control) than any human.
- Surprisingly, robots can be more delicate.

Sense, monitor and control

In the early hours of Sunday 4 March 2001, a bomb disposal vehicle was called to the headquarters of the BBC in London. Eyewitnesses describe what happened.

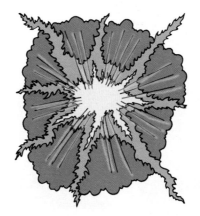

"Just after midnight, a bomb disposal vehicle drove up. The robot stayed close to the taxi. It fired something into the taxi. I think it was to open it up to see what was inside."

"I don't know if it was triggered by the robot firing a second time or if the bomb exploded early, but it was a spectacular ball of fire. The car park we were in shook from the force of the blast. Bits of the robot flew about 80 yards away."

"This was all that was left of the taxi next morning."

The advantages of using a robot in this case are obvious.

Among other things, this robot had a sensor which was able to detect (or sense) tiny amounts of explosive material.

The robots and dummies mentioned here all contain electronic devices which are able to *sense*, *monitor* and *control* the machine or environment in which they are fitted.

Incubators in hospital special-care baby units sense the temperature, monitor it to make sure it does not go too high or too low, and control it with a heater if necessary.

TASKS

1 Not every electronic device is used as dramatically as the bomb disposal robot. Your home and your school both contain many electronic devices which are able to sense, monitor and control the machines or environment in which they are fitted.

Choose a machine in your home or school and explain in general terms:
a what is being sensed
b how it is being monitored
c how it is controlled.

A premature baby is kept alive thanks to the electronic components that monitor and control the incubator in which it spends the first weeks of its life. A premature baby has not developed the mechanisms it needs to control its body temperature (such as sweating or shivering).

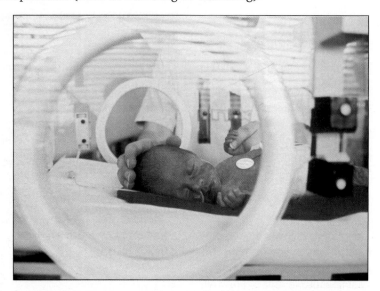

The temperature is measured with a thermistor. A processor analyses the data. A heater is automatically switched on if the baby is too cold. All of the control systems in the incubator are run from the mains electricity supply.

Components of electronic systems

There are four parts to this electronic system:

- the power source is from the mains electricity supply
- the **input component** is the thermistor, which measures the temperature
- the **processor** is a special computer, which is programmed to control the temperature
- the **output component** is the heating element.

All electronic systems have these four parts to them, but with different components.

a Bill has a new portable laptop computer. Which part of the system is:
- **the mouse**
- **the battery**
- **the printer?**

b What other component of the laptop is an input component?

Monitoring motorists

Almost all motorists are familiar with the radar speed cameras that are found at the side of the road, and the portable 'radar guns' used by the police. In many areas, motorists are now being told exactly how fast they are travelling towards a speed monitor. In the West Midlands, drivers on some motorways are shamed by having their registration numbers digitally photographed and displayed as well.

In these examples, the input component is a radar gun, which detects motion. The output component is the display.

c Which type of speed check device uses a battery as a power source?

d Which type of speed check device does not have a camera?

Motorists have to pay a Congestion Charge if they drive into Central London between Mondays and Fridays. If they do not pay this charge, they are fined.

Digital cameras set up throughout the area can read the number plates of cars. These cameras are linked up to a central computer that can identify the name and address of the car owner. The driver has until midnight to pay the charge, otherwise a large fine is automatically sent to the address of the car owner.

A motorist can pay the charge in a number of ways including:
- buying tickets from a machine in shops, garages and car parks
- by e-mail
- by telephone
- by text message.

e How are electronic components used to collect the Congestion Charge?

TASKS

1 A garden centre wants to water the plants in the greenhouse automatically at night.
   a What will be used for the input component, the power source, the processor and the output component?
   b Use the components to build an electronic circuit and test it.

2 **Starting blocks**
   Portfolio Unit 3 CD-ROM

5.20 Electrical properties

The overhead power lines that distribute electricity around the country are made of aluminium.

Most electrical wires are made from copper because copper is 1.5 times better at conducting electricity than aluminium. But aluminium is less dense than copper:

- density of aluminium = 2.7 g/cm^3
- density of copper = 8.9 g/cm^3.

a A copper cable with a cross-section of 5 cm^2 and an aluminium cable with cross-section of 8 cm^2 conduct electricity equally well. Show that the copper cable is about twice the mass of the aluminium cable. (Hint: calculate the mass of a 1 cm length of each cable.)

b How does the fact that the aluminium cable is lighter affect the positioning of pylons?

The cost of the cables must also be considered. The graph shows how the cost of aluminium (Al) has varied this century, compared to the cost of copper (Cu).

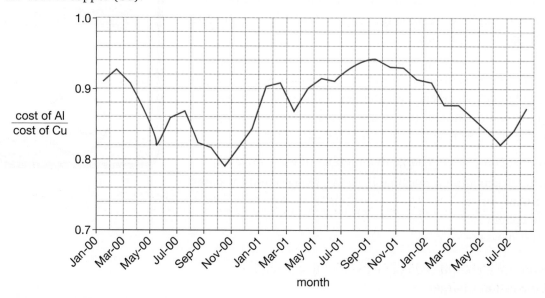

c What conclusion can you make about the cost of aluminium?

Resistance

Scientists usually measure the **resistance** of wires instead of measuring how well they conduct.

They use a circuit like the one on the right.

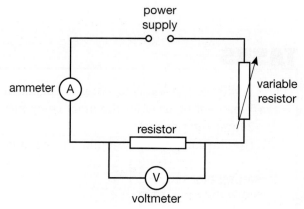

There is an equation that links resistance, **voltage** and **current**:

$$resistance = \frac{voltage}{current}$$

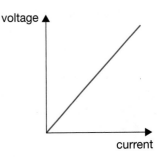

d What is the unit of voltage?

e What is the unit of current?

Resistance is measured in ohms (Ω). The lower the resistance, the better the conductor.

The circuit can be used to find the voltage–current characteristics for a resistor.

The values of voltage and current are plotted on a graph.

To measure resistance, you do not need to use a variable resistor.

f A car headlamp bulb is connected to a 12 V car battery. When it is switched on, a current of 2 A passes through the filament. What is the resistance of the filament?

g The rear lamp of the same car has a current of only 1.2 A passing through the filament. What is the resistance of the filament in the rear lamp?

TASKS

1 The graph at the top of the page shows the voltage–current characteristics for a resistor. Use a similar circuit to the one opposite to investigate the voltage–current characteristics for:
   a a lamp
   b a diode (put it in the circuit both ways round)
   c a thermistor.

2 You already know that the material of a wire affects its resistance. Investigate how the length and the diameter of a wire affect its resistance.

3 **Heater**
   Portfolio Unit 1

4 **Components**
   Portfolio Unit 1

 **More questions**

5.21 Optical devices

Pinhole camera

The simplest optical device is the pinhole camera.

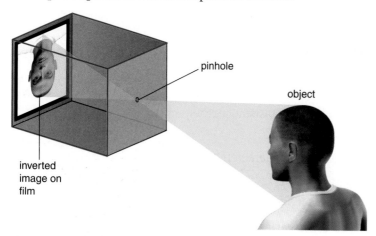

pinhole

object

inverted
image on
film

A light-proof box has a light-sensitive film in the back. In the front is a very small pinhole. Light travels in straight lines so an upside-down image is formed on the film.

Not very much light enters through the pinhole, so the camera has to be left stationary for a long time. If the hole is made any bigger, more light can get through but the image becomes blurred.

Lens camera

The cameras we use everyday for taking photographs have a convex lens to focus the light onto the film.

Light from a distant object converges to a focus.

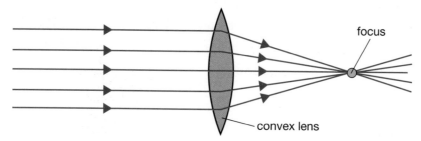

focus

convex lens

The distance from the lens to the focus is called the **focal length**. If you want to take a picture of something that is closer to the camera, the image is not formed at the focus.

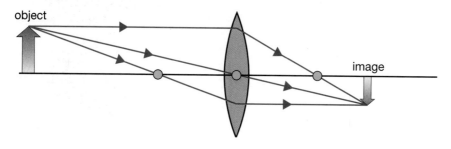

object

image

Most cameras have lenses which move in and out, decreasing or increasing the distance between the lens and the film.

a Patrick takes a picture of some distant mountains and then of a group of friends gathered nearby. Does he need to increase or decrease the distance of the lens from the film?

Simple microscope – magnifying glass

A magnifying glass is sometimes called a simple microscope.

When the object is closer to the lens than the focal length, a **virtual** image is formed. Unlike a **real** image, a virtual image cannot be projected onto a screen.

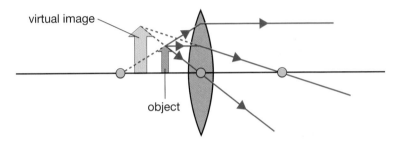

b How does the size of the image in a magnifying glass compare to the size of the object?

Compound microscope

The microscopes we use in the laboratory are compound microscopes. They have two lenses.

The first lens forms an enlarged, real image inside the focal length of the eyepiece. The eyepiece acts as a magnifying glass.

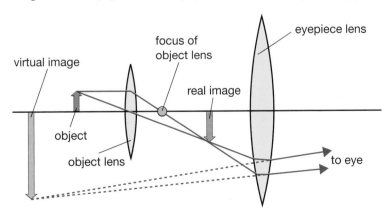

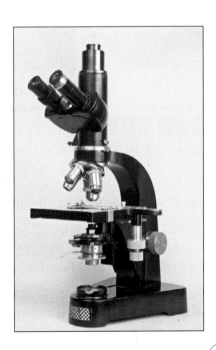

Electromagnetic spectrum

The **electromagnetic spectrum** is a family of *transverse waves* (waves that bob up and down like water waves) that travel at the speed of light.

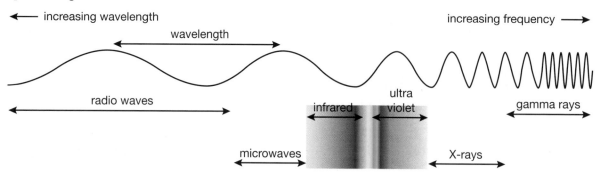

← increasing wavelength

increasing frequency →

wavelength

radio waves

microwaves

infrared

ultra violet

X-rays

gamma rays

The **wavelength** of a wave is the distance between two points on adjacent waves having the same displacement. (Here 'displacement' means the height above the base level or average position of the wave point.) The **frequency** of a wave is the number of waves passing a point each second.

Gamma rays and X-rays have the shortest wavelengths of between 0.000 000 001 mm and 0.000 001 mm. Microwaves and radio waves have wavelengths ranging from 1 mm to more than a kilometre. Frequencies range from 100 000 Hz radio waves to in excess of 10 000 000 000 000 000 000 000 Hz for the highest frequency gamma rays.

Most waves within the spectrum can be used for communication.

Radio waves

Radio waves are used for communicating over short and long distances. Radio waves behave much like light. They can be reflected from solid objects, such as hills or tall buildings.

Radio waves are **refracted** as they pass through different densities within the Earth's atmosphere and reflected by the ionosphere layer.

Radio waves also spread out as they pass obstacles such as hills. Longer-wavelength waves spread out more than the shorter-

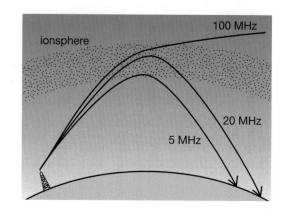

ionosphere

100 MHz

20 MHz

5 MHz

wavelength waves. This means that a house in the shadow of a hill may be able to receive good quality long-wave reception, poor quality medium-wave reception and no VHF reception.

good LW reception

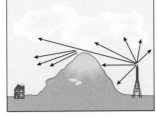
poor MW reception

no VHF reception

Microwaves

Microwaves have a shorter wavelength than radio waves.

a Why may a house that receives VHF radio signals not receive a mobile phone signal?

Microwaves are used to communicate with spacecraft and to transmit satellite television pictures. This is because the transmitter and receiver are in *line of sight*.

b Suggest what is meant by line of sight and explain why this means microwaves are suitable for communicating with spacecraft.

Infrared

Infrared radiation is used as a remote control device for such things as home entertainment centres, computer mice, opening garage doors or gates. Special cameras are used to detect infrared radiation from warm bodies such as people or other animals. Infrared radiation can help fire fighters locate unconscious people, or soldiers on the battlefield.

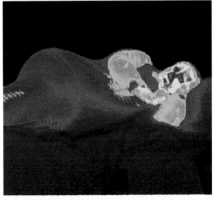
This image shows temperature variation within a human while he is asleep.

Visible light

Optical fibres are very thin fibres of glass that trap light inside them. Communication signals are coded and transmitted as pulses of light along the fibre. A single fibre can transmit thousands of simultaneous signals. Optical fibres are used for telephone communication and transmission of data between computers.

 More on working waves CD-ROM

Case Study: Car technician

Interests and qualifications

Christopher left school six years ago with nine GCSEs, including Double Award Science.

When he was at school, he had no idea what he wanted to do as a job. When choosing his options, he decided on a broad course of study. This meant that he had a wide range of possible career paths open to him. He has always been interested in cars, so during his last year spent his work-experience week at a local garage. This finally decided his future.

After leaving school, Christopher spent a year at college studying Motor Vehicle Engineering. He spent the next year dividing his time between college and the garage where he now works. At the end of this training he gained NVQ levels 1, 2 and 3.

Further qualifications

For the last four years, he has served his apprenticeship at a local family-run garage that has a Renault dealership. He says he feels very much part of the family and they speak highly of him.

Christopher has recently qualified as an MOT tester. This means that he can carry out the annual check on vehicles to make sure they are roadworthy. He also holds a first aid qualification.

As cars get more high-tech, Renault expect specialist car-technicians to service and maintain the vehicles, so Christopher is soon starting an intensive Renault training programme. He will learn to trace faults in a car using a computer.

At school, he did not realise the relevance of the science he was being taught. But if he is changing a brake pad, adjusting the steering, topping up the radiator or fitting an exhaust, he knows he is applying the science he learned every day.

1 What are the disadvantages of choosing a narrow course of study at GCSE?

2 What is the purpose of the MOT test?

3 Why is it important for car technicians to have specialist training in one make of vehicle?

4 Christopher uses a computer in his work. Suggest one thing he uses the computer for.

1 Lee works down a mine.

He knows that coal is one example of a fossil fuel.

a Name **two** other examples of fossil fuels. [2]

b One result of burning fossil fuels is the production of acid rain.
 i What gas is mainly responsible for acid rain? [1]
 ii What effect does acid rain have on the environment? [1]

c One of the gases produced when fossil fuels burn is known as a greenhouse gas because it contributes to the *greenhouse effect*.
 i Which gas is known as a greenhouse gas? [1]
 ii What is meant by the term *greenhouse effect*? [1]

d Sixty years ago, steam trains were a common sight. Some people think that they should return. Use your knowledge of fuel reserves to explain why. [2]

e Copy and complete this equation for the reaction between methane and oxygen when there is a good supply of oxygen.

methane + oxygen → _____ + _____ [2]

f Copy and complete this equation for the reaction between butane and oxygen when there is a poor supply of oxygen.

butane + oxygen → _____ + _____ [2]

2 People choose different fuels for different jobs. Suggest a suitable fuel for each of these jobs. Give a reason for each of your choices.
 a Open fire in the lounge of a large hotel. [2]
 b Barbecue at the beach. [2]
 c Gas cooker in a caravan. [2]

3 Some people are worried about radioactive waste from power stations.
 a How is low level liquid waste disposed of? [1]
 b What happens to waste which is very radioactive? [3]

4 Suggest **four** properties that the ideal energy resource used at an electricity generating station should have. [4]

5 Mrs Singh has a coal fire in her house. She uses 5 kg of coal while the fire is alight. The energy released into the room is the same as if she had a 2 kW electric fire on for 4 hours.
 The total energy stored in 1 kg of coal is 8 kWh.
 a What is the total energy (in kWh) stored in the 5 kg of fuel? [2]
 b How much energy is released into the room while the fire is alight? [2]
 c What is the efficiency of the fire? [3]

6 Some energy resources are *renewable*. Some are *non-renewable*.

   a Which of the following energy resources are renewable?

     coal   natural gas   oil

     sun   tide   waves   wind

     wood   [4]

   b What are the disadvantages of using the tide as an energy resource? [1]

7 Vinotter High School is having a new office block built.

   a Explain how the builders can reduce energy loss by:

     i conduction [3]

     ii convection. [3]

   b Mr Down is the energy-efficiency officer at the school. He asks the builders to put shiny foil behind all radiators. Explain how this helps to keep the building warm in winter and cool in summer. [3]

8 The pie-chart shows, by percentages, the energy resources used by a country.

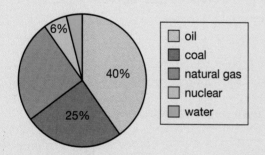

   a What percentage of the energy resources used comes from natural gas? [1]

   b What percentage of the energy resources used comes from water? [1]

   c What percentage of the energy resources used comes from non-renewable resources? [1]

9 The owners of this house want to generate their own electricity using a wind turbine and solar cells.

   a i Where should they site the wind turbine? [1]

     ii Explain the reason for your choice. [1]

     iii What problems are there in generating electricity using a wind turbine? [1]

   b i Where should they site the solar cells? [1]

     ii Explain the reason for your choice. [1]

     iii What problems are there in generating electricity using solar cells? [1]

   c There is a river flowing down the hill behind the house.

     i Suggest how this could be used to generate electricity. [2]

     ii What advantage does using the river have over using the wind or the Sun to generate electricity? [1]

10 The diagram shows what happens during nuclear fission in a nuclear power station.

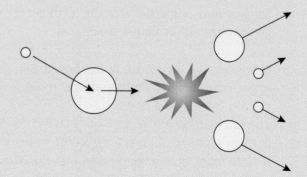

a Copy and complete the sentences. Choose words from this list.

electrons　　**energy**　　**hydrogen**
neutrons　　**uranium**

During nuclear fission, small particles called _____ collide with atoms of _____. These atoms are then unstable and split into smaller atoms and more _____. A lot of _____ is also produced. [4]

b Water in the boilers of the power station is heated and steam is produced. What device in the power station is driven by the steam? [1]

c What device in the power station produces electricity? [1]

11 Mr Marples is the transport manager of a large delivery company. He wants to save money on buying antifreeze. The vans have been using a mixture which is 60% antifreeze, 40% water. He looks at a graph which shows how the freezing point of water varies with antifreeze concentration.

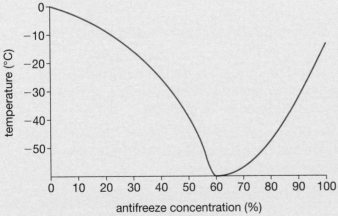

Freezing points of water and antifreeze solution.

a What temperature does water freeze at when the concentration of antifreeze is 50%? [1]

b The lowest ever temperature recorded in the United Kingdom was −27.2°C at Braemar, Grampian Region, Scotland, on 10th January 1982.
  i What concentration would you suggest Mr Marples uses for the fleet of vans? [1]
  ii Explain the reasons for your suggestion. [1]

c Ernie, a driver, suggests using pure antifreeze in the van cooling system, to give maximum protection. Why is this not a sensible idea? [2]

12 An electric toaster used in a hotel dining room is designed to work when the voltage is 250 V and the current is 10 A.

a Calculate the resistance of the heating elements in the toaster. [4]

b The power rating of the toaster is 2.5 kW and the heating elements are switched on constantly while breakfast is being served from 7.00 until 10.00. Electricity costs 8p per unit. How much does it cost the hotel to make the breakfast toast? [3]

195

Case study: Monitoring air pollution

Bill works for the local council. His job is to look after a number of air-pollution monitoring sites around the town. The council has two types of air monitoring equipment: non-automatic and automatic.

Non-automatic monitoring is carried out using diffusion tubes.

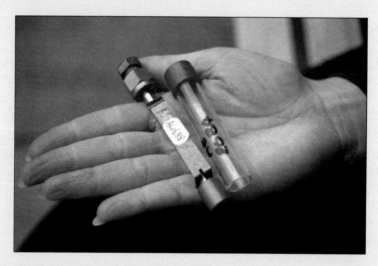

It is Bill's job to put sets of this apparatus in different locations around the town. In the apparatus air is drawn through the tube over a period of days or weeks. Bill visits each monitoring station regularly to make sure the apparatus is working correctly. Then he collects the samples and takes them back to the laboratory to be analysed.

From his results Bill knows the concentration of nitrogen dioxide, sulfur dioxide, ozone and benzene in the air at each location.

The council also has three automatic monitoring stations, set up in permanent locations. These take measurements of air pollution continuously. The data is sent through a telephone line each hour and stored on a computer.

Nitrogen dioxide is a pollutant gas that comes from car exhausts. The table shows how the nitrogen dioxide measurements from the three permanent locations around the town have changed over a period of six years.

	2000	2001	2002	2003	2004	2005
Location	Annual mean, $\mu g/m^3$	Annual mean, $\mu g/m^3$	Annual mean, $\mu g/m^3$	Annual mean, $\mu g/m^3$	Annual mean, $\mu g/m^3$	Annual mean, $\mu g/m^3$
Bath Road	23.2	26.4	28.5	28.8	29.9	32.8
Kent Avenue	22.9	21.3	21.9	22.1	21.5	21.4
Windsor Road	43.7	43.9	37.1	31.3	30.8	29.4

1 What advantage is there in using:
   a automatic monitoring stations
   b non-automatic monitoring stations?

2 Why does Bill visit each non-automatic site regularly while it is in use?

3 Why does Bill have to take samples from these sites back to the laboratory?

4 Look at the data in the table above for nitrogen dioxide air pollution.
   a The concentrations of nitrogen dioxide at Bath road increases during the six years it was monitored.
      Suggest what may have caused this increase.
   b A bypass opened in 2002 takes traffic away from some streets in the town.
      Use information in the table to suggest the name of one of these streets.

5 In addition to nitrogen dioxide, what other pollutants can be measured using Bill's diffusion tube apparatus?

6.1 What's in the air?

How often do we think about the air around us? Every day each of us breathes in and out about 15 000 litres of air. Without the oxygen in this air we would quickly die.

Air contains a mixture of gases.

Gas	Percentage in dry air
nitrogen	78
oxygen	21
carbon dioxide	0.03

The air also contains noble gases such as argon, and varying amounts of water vapour. On cold mornings some of the water vapour condenses to form mist.

a Why is water vapour not included in the table showing percentages of gases in the air?

Protection for life

The carbon dioxide in our atmosphere traps heat energy from the sun. This is called the greenhouse effect, and is essential for all life on the planet. Without the greenhouse effect the Earth would be too cold for life to survive.

About one fifth of the air is oxygen. When we breathe, some of this oxygen is absorbed into our blood stream. This oxygen is used in the process of respiration to provide us with the energy we need to live.

Plants absorb energy from the sun. They use this energy to convert carbon dioxide and water into glucose in the process called photosynthesis. During this process oxygen is released into the air.

The carbon dioxide and oxygen levels in our atmosphere remained constant for thousands of years. A balance was achieved between the carbon dioxide removed and oxygen added during photosynthesis, and the oxygen removed and carbon dioxide added during respiration.

This balance in the gases in our atmosphere is essential for the continuation of life on the Earth.

b Why is it essential for the air to contain a small percentage of carbon dioxide?

The air is changing

Man's activities over the past century have changed our atmosphere.

The burning of more and more fossil fuels has increased the percentage of carbon dioxide in the air. This has in turn increased the greenhouse effect, causing global warming.

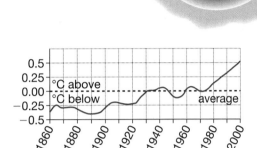

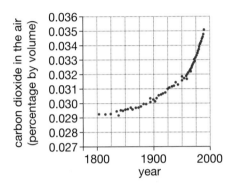

Incomplete combustion of fossil fuels releases unburned hydrocarbons and minute particles of carbon (called particulates) into the air. This may cause an increase in the number of people with asthma and other breathing difficulties.

c Describe one bad effect of increased traffic on our roads.

Monitoring the air

Today scientists measure the amount of gases and particulates in the air.

They monitor how our activities are changing the air around us. We can then take measures to reduce the effect we have on the composition of the atmosphere and to help us stay healthy.

Weather balloon being released by a meteorologist

TASKS

1 What should we do to prevent more changes to our atmosphere in the future?

Write a list of measures that the government could take to make sure that we do not continue to make harmful changes to the air around us.

2 **A report on how science is used in the workplace**
Portfolio Unit 3

CD-ROM

It may seem to us that the Earth is unchanging. The mountains and valleys that we live in appear to remain the same as years go by. Yet changes are taking place, even if some are very slow.

Moving plates

The Earth's **crust** is made of huge plates that float on the liquid **mantle** beneath them. The plates move at a speed of one or two centimetres each year. This map shows the boundaries where one plate meets another.

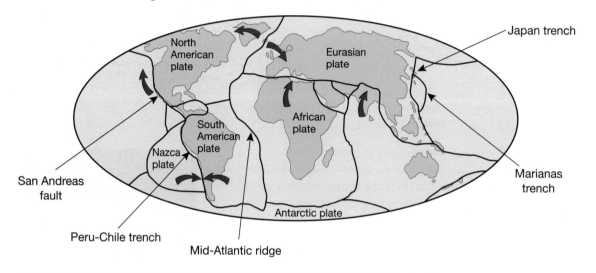

North American plate

Eurasian plate

Japan trench

San Andreas fault

South American plate

Nazca plate

African plate

Marianas trench

Peru-Chile trench

Antarctic plate

Mid-Atlantic ridge

Sudden changes

Where the plates meet, changes can take place very quickly. Where one plate is sliding against another, movement is opposed by friction. Pressure may build up until a sudden movement of perhaps several metres takes place. This is an *earthquake*. If this happens at a plate boundary under the sea, the sudden movement can cause a tidal wave, called a *tsunami*.

a Why do the plates not move smoothly past each other?

The movement of one plate against another can generate enough heat to melt some of the rocks. Along the plate boundaries molten rock may be released through the sudden eruption of *volcanoes*.

Where plates meet head-on, over a period of millions of years the rock may be pushed upwards to create mountains. The Himalayas were formed in this way.

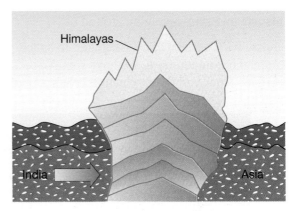

This process is still taking place. The highest mountain on Earth, Mount Everest, is getting higher by a few centimetres each year!

The Earth's land masses, called *continents*, sit on the plates. Movement of the plates results in movement of the continents. This is called **continental drift**.

The diagram shows how the shapes of today's continents fit together like pieces of a jig-saw puzzle. This shows that they were once joined, but over millions of years have moved apart.

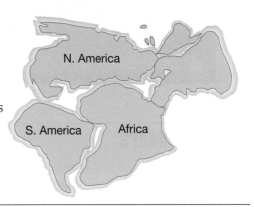

Monitoring plate movement

Earth scientists measure the speed of plate movement by monitoring how rapidly a plate moves relative to the plate next to it. One method uses the Global Positioning System (GPS), which consists of 24 satellites. Satellite signals are recorded by GPS receivers on the ground. This enables the position of markers at each plate boundary to be mapped daily.

Scientists also detect where and when earthquakes occur. They use sensitive measuring equipment to monitor even the smallest Earth tremor.

TASKS

1 A friend does not believe that the Earth's crust is made of plates.
  How could you convince him that it is?

2 Why is it important to measure and record small Earth tremors?

The sky above us has fascinated us ever since the first man appeared on Earth. The patterns of the stars in the sky have been given names such as Plough and Orion. At first, we thought that Earth was at the centre of everything, with the Sun, Moon, planets and stars revolving around us.

Today, with telescopes on Earth and in space, we have seen and understand much more. We have sent spacecraft to explore other planets. However, the fascination of what might still be 'out there' remains.

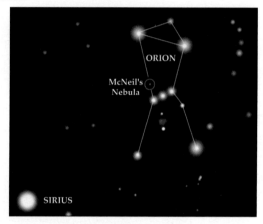

Orion

An astronomer looking at the night sky.

Our neighbours

There are nine planets in our solar system. They orbit around a fiery ball of glowing gas called the Sun. Mercury, Venus, Earth and Mars are the 'inner planets'. Jupiter, Saturn, Uranus, Neptune and Pluto are the 'outer planets'. Small rocks called **asteroids** also orbit the Sun. Most are found in a belt between Mars and Jupiter.

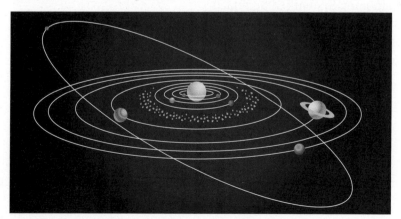

Astronomers have recently discovered other bodies orbiting beyond Pluto. Sedna, for example, is a **planetoid** and was discovered in 2003. Also discovered in 2003, but not announced until 2005, is a planet given a temporary name of 2003UB313. At first scientists thought it was smaller than Pluto, but now they think it is much larger.

Earth is not the only planet to have a moon. Pluto is smaller than our moon but it has a moon, Charon, which is half the size of Pluto.

The asteroid Ida is only 56 km long and it too has a moon, Dactyl, only 1.5 km across.

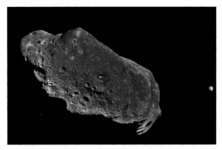
Asteroid Ida and its moon Dactyl.

TASKS

a Which planet has a day length which is longer than its year?
b Which other planet most resembles Earth?
c How does the average surface temperature of the planets vary with distance from the Sun?
d Most asteroids take between 3 and 10 years to orbit the Sun. The asteroid Eros only takes 1.76 years. Suggest why astronomers are studying the path of this asteroid very carefully.

planet	diameter in km	average distance from Sun in millions of km	time to orbit Sun (year length) in units Earth	time to spin on axis (day length) in Earth units	average surface temperature in °C	major moons
Mercury	4800	58	88 days	58.6 days	day 350 night −170	none
Venus	12 200	108	225 days	243 days	465	none
Earth	12 800	150	365.25 days	24 h	15	Moon
Mars	7000	228	687 days	24 h 37 m	−23	Phobos Deimos
Jupiter	143 000	778	11.9 years	9 h 50 m	−150	Io Europa Ganymede Callisto 12 others
Saturn	120 000	1427	29.5 years	10 h 37 m	−180	Titan Janus Epimetheus at least 16 others
Uranus	49 000	2870	84.0 years	17 h 14 m	−210	Ariel Miranda Oberon Titania 11 others
Neptune	50 000	4497	164.8 years	16 h 3 m	−220	Triton 7 others
Pluto	4000	5913	248.0 years	6.4 days	−230	Charon

6.4 The Universe

Our solar system is just one of millions of star systems in our galaxy – the Milky Way.

The star nearest to our Sun, which you can also see with the naked eye, is Alpha Centauri. Light from Alpha Centauri takes just over four years to reach us. We say that the distance to Alpha Centauri is just over four **light years**. A light year is a unit of distance and is a measure of how far light travels in one year.

The Milky Way

1 light year = 9 460 700 000 000 km approximately

The Milky Way is one of many millions of galaxies in the Universe. The galaxy closest to the Milky Way is Andromeda. Light from the centre of Andromeda takes over two million years to reach us.

The farthest objects we can see in the sky with the aid of telescopes are *quasars*. Light from them takes about 12 billion years to reach us. This supports the idea that the Universe is at least that old.

Andromeda galaxy

The Big Bang

Scientists believe that the Universe was formed about 15 billion years ago. All of the matter from the Universe was concentrated at a point. The temperature was a staggering 1000 million million million million °C. In the smallest fraction of a second, there was an enormous explosion – the **Big Bang**. The force of gravity became identifiable. All particles were created. The Universe expanded and cooled.

After just one ten-millionth of a second, the temperature had dropped to below one million million °C. It took just three seconds for hydrogen and helium to form, but a further 400 000 years before any other atoms were formed. Stars did not start to shine for 200 million years.

a How do quasars help to confirm the age of the Universe?

What next?

At the moment, the Universe is continuing to expand. But it is expanding at a slower rate. What happens next depends on how much matter there is in the Universe. At the moment, scientists believe that the Universe will continue to expand, but at an ever slowing rate.

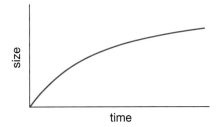

If there is more matter than we know about, then the Universe will expand to reach a finite size.

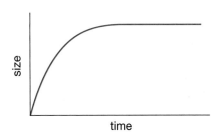

If there is a lot more matter than we know about, then the Universe will reach a maximum size and then start to get smaller. Eventually, everything will once again be concentrated at a single point. Scientists call this collapse the **Big Crunch**.

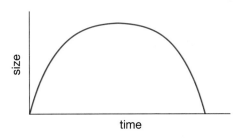

Other life forms

The odds are that somewhere out there are conditions similar to those on Earth which could allow life to develop. Scientists have sent radio signals into space to see if there is any reply. It may take 50 000 years before we get any answer.

Spaceships containing pictures representing life on Earth have also been sent.

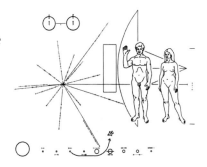

TASKS

1 You have the opportunity to send five items, which can be objects, photographs or drawings, into deep space. You hope that another life form will find them. What five things would you send? Why would you send them?

2 Use the Internet or other source to find out the distances to the stars in one of the constellations.

Case Study: Becoming an astronaut

Serious about science

Helen Sharman was born in Sheffield on 30 May 1963. She went to local primary schools and then to Jordanthorpe Comprehensive. She took Physics, Chemistry and Biology as three separate subjects at the end of Year 11. She continued her studies into the sixth-form studying Mathematics, Physics, Chemistry and General Studies. In 1984 she gained a degree in Chemistry at Sheffield University.

Her first job was with a company that made cathode ray tubes for televisions. In 1986 Helen began studying for a PhD at Birkbeck College in London.

From chocolate to space

In August 1987, Helen changed jobs. She began working for Mars Confectionery. Part of her job was to study the chemical and physical properties of chocolate! One evening, she was driving home from the factory when she heard an advert on the radio: 'Astronaut wanted – no experience necessary.' Anyone interested had to be British, aged 21–40, with a science background. They also had to be very fit and able to learn Russian. Helen jotted down the telephone number whilst waiting for traffic lights to change! The thought of going into space and experiencing weightlessness was too good an opportunity to miss.

First Briton in space

More than 13 000 people applied. Helen was chosen as one of the final four candidates on the Soviet space mission Project Juno. There were weeks of more tests. In the end, she was one of the final two candidates. There were still another 18 months of training in Moscow. Finally, on 18 May 1991 Helen became the first Briton in space. She spent 8 days at the Mir Space Station conducting scientific experiments.

After her return to Earth, Helen has continued to work as one of the country's leading scientists. She has given lectures all around the world. She has presented many science-based radio and television programmes, many of them aimed at school students. Her hobbies include sports and motorbiking.

Helen Sharman has described her background as 'ordinary'. Most people would agree that her achievement as the first British person in space is quite extraordinary!

1 A cathode ray tube is used to produce the picture in a television. Where else are cathode ray tubes used?

2 Suggest why an astronaut has to be very fit.

3 Some people say "You feel weightless because there is no gravity in space." Explain what is wrong with this statement.

1   Fill in the gaps in this table about the gases in the air around us.

gas	percentage in dry air
argon	1
	0.04
nitrogen	21

[3]

2   Analysis of a sample of air from a town centre showed the presence of the following substances.

   **argon   carbon dioxide   carbon monoxide   carbon particles
   nitrogen   nitrogen dioxide   oxygen   sulfur dioxide**

   a   Which of these substances are considered pollutants?
   b   Which of these substances is a solid?
   c   Which of these substances come from car exhausts?   [8]

3   Arrange the following in order, starting with the smallest.

   asteroid   galaxy   planet   star   Universe   [4]

4   The diagram represents the orbits of planets in our Solar System.

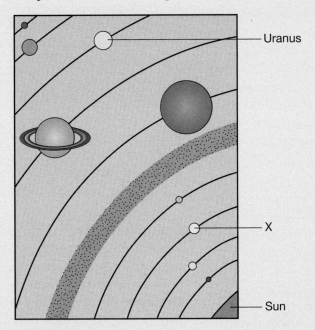

   a   What is the name of the star at the centre of our Solar System?   [1]
   b   Between which two planets are most asteroids found?   [1]
   c   There is a natural satellite orbiting the planet labelled **X**. What is the name of
       the satellite?   [1]
   d   Name the two planets further from the Sun than Uranus.   [2]
   e   Our Solar System is part of a galaxy. What is the name of the galaxy? [1]

5   What name has been given to the explosion that scientists believe caused the
    start of the Universe?   [1]

6 How is life on Earth dependent on the greenhouse effect [2]

7 During the past 100 years the concentration of carbon dioxide in the air increased.
   a What caused this increase? [1]
   b What effect may this increase have on the life on the Earth? [1]

8 The table shows the results of air monitoring for pollutants in two locations.

pollutant	concentration in $\mu g/m^3$	
	location A	location B
carbon monoxide	9	22
carbon particles	0	38
nitrogen dioxide	15	42
sulfur dioxide	38	24

   a Which location is most likely to be the centre of a large town? [1]
   b Suggest an explanation for the sulfur dioxide results. 2]

9 What evidence supports the idea that the Earth's crust is made of moving plates? [2]

10 Earthquakes are caused by sudden movements of the plates that make up the Earth's crust.
   a How are these plates able to move? [2]
   b Why do the plates not move smoothly past each other? [1]
   c Why do the plates sometimes make a 'jerking' movement that causes an earthquake? [1]

11 How can movement of the Earth's plates create mountain ranges? [2]

12 There are several theories about how the Universe will change over time.
   These theories depend on the total mass of matter in the Universe.
   At the moment, scientists believe the Universe will continue to expand, but at a slowing rate.
   a What do they expect to happen if there is more matter than calculated? [1]
   b What do they expect to happen if there is a lot more matter than calculated? [1]

13 Explain what is meant by the statement 'Alpha Centauri is 4 light years away'. [2]

14 Every car that is more than three years old has to undergo a Ministry of Transport test each year. Part of this test is to monitor the concentration of pollutant gases released from the exhaust system of the car.
   a The level of carbon dioxide in gases released from cars is not measured as part of this test. Suggest why. [1]
   b Which pollutant gases are likely to be present and therefore need to be measured in the fumes released from a car exhaust system? [3]
   c For one of the gases you have suggested in part a, describe how it is harmful when released into the atmosphere. [2]
   d Suggest why cars under three years old are not tested. [1]
   e Suggest why cars over three years old should be tested each year. [1]

15 To see how carbon dioxide levels in the atmosphere are changing, scientists measure the percentage of carbon dioxide in air sampled in different places.
   They need to compare their results with data for carbon dioxide levels in the past.
   Data for the past century is available because scientists were recording data then, but data much older than that is not readily available.
   One way to obtain useful information is to study ice cores from the poles.
   Explain how the study of ice cores can provide information about carbon dioxide percentages in the air centuries ago. [4]

16 Seismologists are scientists who collect data about movements of the plates that make up the Earth's crust.

   a Describe how these scientists collect this data. [2]

   b Why is the collection of this data useful? [2]

17 Some changes to the Earth's surface occur slowly over time, while others happen very quickly.

   a i Give one example of a change that has taken place slowly over time. [1]

      ii What evidence shows that this change has taken place? [1]

   b Give two examples of changes that take place quickly. [2]

18 There are air-monitoring stations all around the country. They monitor different pollutants. Most monitoring stations are in fixed locations in towns and cities, and they measure air quality continuously.

   a Why are there more monitoring stations in towns and cities? [1]

   b Suggest two air pollutants they might measure. [2]

   c What is the advantage of fixed monitoring stations rather than mobile ones that might sample air in different places? [1]

   d Why is it important to monitor air pollution continuously? [1]

19 The table gives concentration figures of nitrogen oxides at a site in a city at 4-hour intervals on 7th November 2005.

Time of day	Concentration in $\mu g/m^3$
0000 (midnight)	15.0
0400	13.1
0800	23.0
1200	17.6
1600	15.8
2000	16.1
0000	14.9

   a A scientist says that these results show that air pollution reaches a peak twice in each day – once during the morning rush-hour and once during the evening rush-hour.

     Has he sufficient evidence to say this? Explain your answer. [2]

   b The scientist is going to display these results on a grid. Why would it be better to use a bar chart rather than a line graph with the points joined by straight lines? [2]

   c Why could his results be affected by heavy rain? [1]

   d Calculate the average concentration during this period. [2]

   e Scientists would say that the average alone is not enough information. They also give the range – the difference between the highest and the lowest values. What is the range for the table of data? Why is the range important? [2]

20 Use the map on page 200 to explain each of the following observations.

   a There is a range of high mountains that run down the west of South America. [1]

   b South America and Africa are moving apart very slowly. [1]

Units of measure and their symbols

Quantity	Units (symbols)	
mass	kilogram (kg)	gram (g)
	milligram (mg)	microgram (µg)
length	metre (m)	kilometre (km)
	centimetre (cm)	millimetre (mm)
	micrometre (µm)	
volume	cubic metre (m^3)	cubic decimetre (dm^3)
	cubic centimetre (cm^3)	
	litre (l)	millilitre (ml)
time	second (s)	minute (min)
	hour (h)	
temperature	degree Celsius (°C)	
chemical quantity	mole (mol)	
potential difference (voltage)	volt (V)	
current	ampere (A)	milliampere (mA)
resistance	ohm (Ω)	kilohm (kΩ)
	megohm (MΩ)	
force	newton (N)	
energy (work	joule (J)	kilojoule (kJ)
	kilowatt-hour (kWh)	
power	watt (W)	kilowatt (kW)
density	kilogram per cubic metre (kg/m^3 or $kg\,m^{-3}$)	
	gram per cubic centimetre (g/cm^3 or $g\,cm^{-3}$)	
concentration	mole per cubic decimetre (mol/dm^3 or $mol\,dm^{-3}$)	
	gram per cubic decimetre (g/dm^3 or $g\,dm^{-3}$)	

Names and symbols of common elements

Metals		Non-metals	
Element	Chemical symbol	Element	Chemical symbol
Aluminium	Al	Bromine	Br
Barium	Ba	Carbon	C
Calcium	Ca	Chlorine	Cl
Iron	Fe	Fluorine	F
Lead	Pb	Hydrogen	H
Magnesium	Mg	Nitrogen	N
Potassium	K	Oxygen	O
Silver	Ag	Phosphorus	P
Sodium	Na	Silicon	Si
Zinc	Zn	Sulfur	S

Names and formulae of common compounds

Compound	Formula	Compound	Formula
Ammonia	NH_3	Barium chloride	$BaCl_2$
Carbon dioxide	CO_2	Sodium chloride	NaCl
Methane	CH_4	Calcium carbonate	$CaCO_3$
Water	H_2O	Copper carbonate	$CuCO_3$
Hydrochloric acid	HCl	Sodium carbonate	Na_2CO_3
Sulfuric acid	H_2SO_4	Potassium nitrate	KNO_3
Calcium oxide	CaO	Silver nitrate	$AgNO_3$
Iron oxide	Fe_2O_3	Barium sulfate	$BaSO_4$
Lead oxide	PbO	Copper sulfate	$CuSO_4$
Sodium hydroxide	NaOH	Sodium sulfate	Na_2SO_4

Equations and formulae

Biology

Photosynthesis:

$$\text{carbon dioxide} + \text{water} \xrightarrow{\text{light and chlorophyll}} \text{glucose} + \text{oxygen}$$
$$6CO_2 + 6H_2O \rightarrow C_6H_{12}O_6 + 6O_2$$

Respiration in plant cells is the same as that in animal cells with a good supply of oxygen. It is aerobic respiration.

$$\text{glucose} + \text{oxygen} \rightarrow \text{water} + \text{carbon dioxide} + \text{ENERGY}$$
$$C_6H_{12}O_6 + 6O_2 \rightarrow 6CO_2 + 6H_2O$$

Anaerobic respiration does not use oxygen. This anaerobic respiration sometimes takes place in muscles:

$$\text{glucose} \rightarrow \text{lactic acid} + \text{ENERGY}$$
$$C_6H_{12}O_6 \rightarrow 2C_3H_6O_3$$

Anaerobic respiration also takes place in yeast. This process is known as fermentation:

$$\text{glucose} \rightarrow \text{ethanol (alcohol)} + \text{carbon dioxide} + \text{ENERGY}$$
$$C_6H_{12}O_6 \rightarrow 2C_2H_5OH + 2CO_2$$

Chemistry

When calcium carbonate is heated it decomposes into quicklime. This is called thermal decomposition:

$$\text{calcium carbonate (limestone)} \rightarrow \text{calcium oxide (quicklime)} + \text{carbon dioxide}$$
$$CaCO_3 \rightarrow CaO + CO_2$$

The word equation for the reaction between limestone and hydrochloric acid is

$$\text{calcium carbonate} + \text{hydrochloric acid} \rightarrow \text{calcium chloride} + \text{carbon dioxide} + \text{water}$$
$$CaCO_3 + 2HCl \rightarrow CaCl_2 + CO_2 + H_2O$$

Acid rain contains sulfuric acid. It corrodes old buildings made from limestone:

$$\text{calcium carbonate} + \text{sulfuric acid} \rightarrow \text{calcium sulfate} + \text{carbon dioxide} + \text{water}$$
$$CaCO_3 + H_2SO_4 \rightarrow CaSO_4 + CO_2 + H_2O$$

Sodium metal and chlorine gas combine to make sodium chloride:

$$\text{sodium} + \text{chlorine} \rightarrow \text{sodium chloride}$$
$$2Na + Cl_2 \rightarrow 2NaCl$$

Percentage yield compares the actual yield with the theoretical yield:

$$\text{percentage yield} = \frac{\text{actual yield}}{\text{theoretical yield}} \times 100\%$$

Ammonium sulfate is a fertiliser. This is how it is made in the laboratory:

ammonium hydroxide + sulfuric acid $\rightarrow$ ammonium sulfate + water

$$2NH_4OH + H_2SO_4 \rightarrow (NH_4)_2SO_4 + 2H_2O$$

Oxygen is removed from iron oxide to get iron. This is an example of a reduction reaction:

iron oxide + carbon $\rightarrow$ iron + carbon dioxide

$$2Fe_2O_3 + 3C \rightarrow 4Fe + 3CO_2$$

This reaction is what makes self-heating cans heat. It is an exothermic reaction.

calcium oxide + water $\rightarrow$ calcium hydroxide

$$CaO + H_2O \rightarrow Ca(OH)_2$$

Physics

The energy efficiency of a machine is the amount of useful energy that it outputs compared to the total energy input:

$$\text{energy efficiency} = \frac{\text{useful energy output}}{\text{total energy input}}$$

Sometimes it is useful to show energy efficiency as a percentage:

$$\text{percentage energy efficiency} = \frac{\text{useful energy output}}{\text{total energy input}} \times 100\%$$

In a circuit:

$$\text{resistance} = \frac{\text{voltage}}{\text{current}}$$

$$\text{power} = \text{voltage} \times \text{current}$$

Electrical energy in the home is measured in kilowatt hours (kWh):

energy transferred (in kWh) = power rating (in kW) $\times$ time (in h)

cost of electricity = energy transferred (in kWh) $\times$ cost per kWh (in pence)

Glossary

acid rain rain containing acids, caused by emissions from coal-burning power stations

actual yield the mass of a product made during a reaction

adapted fit or possessing features suitable for its environment

aerobic respiration process in which cells use oxygen to break down glucose and release energy

aerosol colloid in which a liquid is dispersed in a gas

agar plate a Petri dish containing agar

allele a genetic instruction received from one parent. Alleles from both parents form a gene

alveoli small air sacs in the lungs

anaerobic respiration process in which cells break down glucose without oxygen

antibiotic a tablet or capsule given to people to kill bacteria in their body

antibody a chemical produced in the human body that kills microorganisms

antiseptic a chemical used to kill microorganisms on the skin and in the mouth

aorta the main artery that carries blood away from the heart out to the rest of the body

arteries blood vessels that carry blood away from the heart

artificial fertilisers chemicals that put more minerals into the soil to make plants grow better

aseptic technique the technique used when working with microorganisms

asteroid small planet-like body revolving round the sun, especially between the orbits of Mars and Jupiter

atom the smallest particle of an element

atria the two upper chambers of the heart

bacterium a type of microorganism. Most are harmless, but many are useful and a few cause diseases such as TB

Big Bang a theory that the Universe began with an explosion about 15 billion years ago

Big Crunch a theory that the Universe may collapse into a single point – the reverse of the Big Bang

bioenergy the energy contained within biomass

biofuel biomass that is burned to release energy

biological control the use of a living organism to control a pest population

biomass the animals and plants on the Earth's surface

blood plasma the pale yellow liquid that forms the fluid part of the blood

bond attraction between chemical units

breathing rate the number of times the body breathes in and out in one minute

brine solution of sodium chloride in water

brittle easy to shatter into pieces

bulk chemicals chemicals made and used in large quantities, e.g. sulfuric acid and ammonia

capillaries tiny blood vessels that connect arteries and veins

carbohydrates energy-giving foods, such as starch and sugar

carrier a person who can pass on a disease but does not suffer from it

catalyst a substance that makes a reaction go more quickly but is not used up in the reaction

cell membrane the outer covering of a cell. In plants, bacteria and fungi, this is covered by the cell wall

cell nucleus the control centre of the cell which contains the organism's genetic information

cell wall the outer covering of the cell in plants, bacteria and fungi

ceramic material made from clay fired in an oven

chlorophyll the chemical that gives plants their green colour. It absorbs the light that the plant needs for photosynthesis

chloroplasts the parts of a plant cell that contain chlorophyll

chromatography method used to separate a mixture of solutes in a solvent

chromosomes tiny threads that carry genes, found inside the nucleus of each cell

clones two or more organisms that are genetically identical

colloid a mixture of substances that do not normally mix

combustion burning in air or oxygen

compete (of organisms) to struggle with each other for resources

composite material made from a combination of two or more materials

compound a substance made by chemically joining two or more elements

condense to change state from gas to liquid, e.g. steam to water

conduction the way in which heat is transferred through a solid

conductor of heat a material that allows heat to pass through it

contagious able to communicate disease

contaminate to add a pollutant or other unwanted material

continental drift the theory that all land was a single unit, and now the continents are parts of that landmass floating around to new positions

continuous phase substance through which another is spread in a colloid

convection the way in which heat is transferred through a liquid or gas

corroded damaged by chemical reaction

corrosive capable of causing a substance to be corroded by chemical reaction

covalent bond attractive bond between chemical units (atoms, molecules, etc.) based on electron sharing instead of an exchange of electrons

crop rotation growing different kinds of crops in the same soil in successive growing seasons

cross-breeding selective breeding across varieties or breeds

crust the top layer of the earth or *lithosphere*, containing large amounts of lighter elements like aluminium and silicon

crystals solid form of a salt containing some water (of crystallisation)

current the flow of charge in a circuit

cytoplasm the liquid or jelly-like material that fills up the cell

decomposition the breaking-up of a compound into smaller compounds or elements

diabetes condition caused by lack of insulin

diaphragm the sheet of muscle below the lungs that moves upwards and downwards to make us breathe

diffusion movement of particles from a place of higher concentration to a place of lower concentration

digested (of large food molecules) broken down into small soluble food molecules

disinfectant chemical used to kill microorganisms, e.g. on work surfaces and in drains and toilets

disperse phase substance spread through another in a colloid

distillation separation of liquids in a mixture by evaporation and condensation

durability ability to last for a long time

efficiency $\dfrac{\text{useful energy output}}{\text{total energy input}}$

electromagnetic spectrum a family of transverse waves travelling at the speed of light

electron negative sub-atomic particle, found in shells around the nucleus of an atom

element a substance that cannot be broken down into another simpler substance

emulsion colloid in which a liquid is dispersed in another liquid

endothermic type of reaction that takes in heat energy from the surroundings

enzyme a catalyst made by living cells

equation a way of representing a reaction using words or symbols

eutrophication process by which ponds, rivers and lakes become enriched with nutrients, eventually leading to the death of organisms in the water

evaporation change of state of a liquid into a gas

exothermic reaction that gives out heat energy to the surroundings

features characteristics of an organism such as *disease resistance* or *brown hair*

fermentation a type of respiration occurring in many microorganisms. It is the process by which yeast makes alcohol and carbon dioxide

fertiliser a compound or mixture of compounds added to soil to aid growth of plants

filament the thin wire in a bulb which glows white hot to produce light

fine chemicals chemicals made and used in small quantities, e.g. dyes or medicines

flame test test used to identify a metal ion by the colour it gives to a flame

flammable burns easily in oxygen or air

flexible easy to bend without breaking

foam colloid in which a gas is dispersed in a liquid

focal length the distance between the principal focus and centre of a lens

food chain 'linear' picture or flowchart showing what eats an organism and what it eats

food web lots of food chains put together, showing that food chains are linked and more than one animal may eat a particular plant or animal

formula way of representing a compound using symbols

fossil fuels fuels produced from the slow decay of dead animals and plants

fraction a mixture, containing a small number of liquids, that has been separated from a mixture containing a large number of liquids

fractional distillation the separation of a mixture of a large number of different liquids (e.g. crude oil) into smaller groups of liquids called fractions

free-range hens hens that are allowed to move freely and are not kept in battery cages

frequency the number of complete waves passing a point in one second

friction a force between two objects sliding against one another

fuel a substance that is burnt to produce a lot of heat energy

fungi a group of organisms including moulds, yeast, blight, mushrooms and toadstools

fungicide a chemical that is used to kill fungi

gel a colloid containing a liquid dispersed in a solid

gene a short section of a chromosome. Each gene is linked to a feature such as eye colour

gene insertion the process of placing a gene into the chromosome of a different organism

generator a device which uses the relative rotation of a magnet and coils of wire to produce electricity

genetic diseases diseases which are inherited

genetic engineering the removal of a gene from one living organism and putting it into another

genetic modification changing the genes of a crop to improve it

global warming theory that the Earth is heating up, particularly because of human activities polluting the environment

greenhouse effect theory that the earth heats up because of increased quantities of certain gases like carbon dioxide and methane in the atmosphere

greenhouse gas a gas, such as carbon dioxide, that contributes to the greenhouse effect

hazardous (of a substance) capable of causing harm

heart rate the number of times the heart beats in one minute

heat exchanger a device that uses the heat from one process to provide heat for another

herbicide a chemical used to control weeds

homeostasis stability of conditions inside the body

hormone a chemical messenger released from various glands and carried in the blood

hydrocarbon compound made from hydrogen and carbon only

hydroelectric power station a power station that uses the kinetic energy of falling water to produce electricity

immiscible a liquid is immiscible when it will not dissolve in another liquid

immunisation the process by which a person is made resistant to disease

inherit to derive characteristics from the parents

inorganic type of compound that does not contain carbon. The only exceptions are carbonates, which can be inorganic

input component a device in an electronic circuit which detects a change

insecticide a chemical used to kill insects

insulation a material that does not easily transfer heat

insulator material that will not allow an electric current to pass through it

insulin a hormone produced in the pancreas. It reduces the level of glucose in the blood

intensive farming a system of farming that uses modern technology to produce maximum yields

ion a chemical unit which has extra electrons or too few electrons, so it carries charge

ionic bond attractive bond between chemical units which involves the transfer of electrons between them

kilowatt-hour a unit of energy used in measuring the amount of electricity consumed in homes and in industry

kinetic energy the energy of a moving object

light year the distance travelled by light in one year

malleable able to be beaten into sheets

mantle the middle layer of the earth, below the crust, which is made largely of heavier elements like magnesium and iron

metal an element with metallic properties

microbiology the study of microorganisms

microorganism an organism too small to be seen properly without a microscope

mineral a compound contained within a rock

mineral element chemical element essential for growth in plants

miscible a liquid is miscible when it will dissolve in another liquid

mixture a combination of different chemical units which are not in a fixed proportion, and can be separated back into the different types of units without using chemical reactions

model a way of representing how an idea or device works

neutralisation reaction between an acid and an alkali (or a metal, metal oxide or carbonate)

neutron sub-atomic particle with no charge, found in the nucleus of an atom

non-renewable energy energy from sources that have taken a very long time to form and cannot quickly be replaced

nuclear fusion the joining together of nuclei of light atoms to form a heavier atom with the release of energy

nucleus centre of an atom, containing protons and neutrons; also central part of a cell, carrying genetic information

ores rocks containing metals or metal compounds

organic an organic compound is a carbon compound other than a carbonate

organic farmers farmers who grow food without the use of chemical fertilisers or pesticides

organic foods foods that have been produced without the use of chemical fertilisers or pesticides

organism any living thing

osmosis the diffusion of water molecules through a partially permeable membrane

output component a device in an electronic circuit whose behaviour is changed by a processor

oxygen debt the oxygen debt is caused by anaerobic respiration and the production of lactic acid. After exercise oxygen is needed to break down the lactic acid

partially permeable membrane a membrane that will let some molecules through, but not others

particulates very small particles

passive smoking taking in smoke (and

suffering risks of disease) because of being around a smoker

penicillin the first antibiotic to be discovered

pest something that is harmful to us, or harmful to the food we eat

pesticide a chemical used to control pests

Petri dish a shallow dish in which microorganisms are grown

pharmaceutical company a firm that researches, develops or manufactures medical drugs

photosynthesis the process by which plants make their own food

pigment substance used to give colour to a material

planetoid one of the larger asteroids

plasticiser substance added to a polymer to alter its properties, usually to make the polymer more flexible

poisonous (of a substance) causing harm or death if eaten or drunk

polymer long-chain molecule built up from a large number of small units, called monomers, joined together by a process called polymerisation

power rating rate at which energy is transferred in an electric circuit

precipitate solid produced when two clear solutions are mixed

predator insects insects that hunt and kill other organisms for food

processed changed from its original form by an industrial method

processor a device that changes the input of an electronic system

products substances made in a chemical reaction

protein type of food needed for growth

proton positive sub-atomic particle, found in the nucleus of an atom

pulse the wave of blood, travelling through arteries, caused by the heart pumping

pulse rate the number of times the pulse is felt in one minute

radiation the way in which heat is transferred without the need for a material

radioactive radioactive materials emit alpha, beta or gamma radiation from the nuclei of their atoms

reactants substances that react together in a chemical reaction

real image an image which can be projected onto a screen

red blood cells blood cells that contain the red pigment haemoglobin, which carries oxygen around the body

refracted light which is 'bent' or changes direction as it passes through different media (like air, glass, water, etc.)

renewable energy energy sources that are constantly available, sometimes known as alternative energy

reprocessing recycling fuel so it can be used again

reserves the known amounts of fossil fuels that exist on Earth

resistance the opposition to the current in an electric circuit

respiration the process by which all living things break down food to release the energy they need to live

rigid hard to bend, not flexible

rock salt mixture of sodium chloride and rock mined from the ground

root hairs the fine 'hairs' on roots where plants absorb water and nutrients from the soil

salt common name for sodium chloride, but also a term used for other products of metal–acid reactions

selective breeding a technique by which farmers breed plants and animals to improve their usefulness

solar cell a device that uses light from the Sun to produce electricity

solar panel a device that uses heat from the Sun to warm water

solute solid that dissolves in a solvent to make a solution

solution result of dissolving a solute in a solvent

solvent a liquid that dissolves a solid, liquid or gas to form a solution

specific heat capacity a measure of the energy transferred when the temperature of 1 kg of a material is changed by 1°C

sterilisation the use of heat to kill microorganisms

suspension mixture of a solid and a liquid in which it is insoluble

sustainable development leaving the planet to the next generation in no worse a state than that in which the present generation found it

symbol shorthand way of representing an element, using one or two letters

synthetic made by humans, not occurring naturally

thermal conductivity a measure of how well a material conducts heat

thermogram a picture formed by recording different temperatures

thorax the cavity in the body above the diaphragm that contains the heart and lungs

tidal barrage a device that uses the incoming and outgoing tides to produce electricity

transparent able to let light pass through

turbine a device that produces rotation

ultraviolet radiation part of the electromagnetic spectrum next to the violet end of the visible spectrum

vaccine a liquid given to people and animals to build up resistance to a disease

vacuole the central, fluid-filled region of a plant cell

valve part of the heart that prevents backflow of blood

veins blood vessels that return blood to the heart

ventricles the two lower chambers of the heart

villi tiny finger-like projections in the small intestine that increase the surface area for absorption

virtual image an image that cannot be projected onto a screen

virus a very small microorganism that causes disease

voltage a measure of the energy transferred in an electric circuit

vulcanising the hardening of rubber using sulfur

wavelength the distance between two successive points of identical displacement on a wave

wind farm a collection of wind turbines

wind turbine a device turned by the wind to produce electricity

yield the amount of product made in a chemical reaction or the amount of grain or other food produced by a crop

Index

environmental scientists 117
enzymes 4–5, 6–7
ethane 107
ethanol (alcohol) 4, 6
eutrophication 26, 39

fermentation 4–5
fertilisers 26–27, 54, 114
fibreglass 127, 175
filament light bulbs 168–171
fine chemicals 116
fired clay 132
fish farming 39
flame test 101
flammable chemicals 107
flexible materials 130
foams 138, 139
focal lengths 188
fossil fuels 148–151, 199
fractional distillation 106
free-range hens 38
frequency (radiowaves) 190
friction 161
food (humans) 74–75, 82–83
food (plants) 14–17
food chains 34
food poisoning 82
food webs 34, 37
fossil fuels 148–151, 199
fuels (*see also* energy) 164–165
    fossil fuels 148–151, 199
    nuclear fuels 152–153
fungi 28, 29, 78
fungicides 30
fusion (nuclear power) 159

galaxies 204
galena 118
gametes 13
gamma rays 190
gases in plants 20–21
gasoline 106
gels 138, 139
gene insertion 48
gene pairs 45
generators (electricity) 162–163
genes 13, 44, 49
genetic diseases 88–89
genetic engineering 48–49
genetics 44–47
glass 130, 133
glass-reinforced plastic 127
Global Positioning System 201
global warming 36
    greenhouse effect 150, 198–9
glucose 15
    fermentation 4
    Penicillium mould 8
    photosynthesis 15
    respiration in humans 60, 61, 74
    respiration in plants 16

GM crops 48–49
gold 96, 136
Great Famine (Ireland) 29
greenhouse effect 150, 198–9
    global warming 36
greenhouses 25

haematite 118
heart rates 68
hearts 70–71
heat exchangers 176–177
herbicides 30, 32
HIV 79
homeostasis 77
hormones 76
humans 58–90
    blood 68–69, 71, 74
    blood sugar level 76–77
    breathing 60–65
    diseases 78–79, 80
    food 74–75, 82–83
    genetic diseases 88–89
    heart 70–71
    immune system 84–85
Huntington's career 88, 89
hydrocarbons 106
hydrochloric acid 102–103, 110
hydroelectric power 156–157
hydrogen 106, 109, 140

immiscible liquids 138
immune system 84–85
immunisation 84–85
incomplete combustion 199
infections 80–81
inheritance 45
inorganic compounds 107
input components 184
insecticides 30
insects 28, 30, 32
insulation (heat) 172-175
insulators (electricity) 132
insulin 48, 76
intensive farming 26, 38–39
    artificial fertilisers 26–27
    pesticides 30–31, 52
intercostal muscles 64
ionic bonds 141
ions 141
iron 99, 118, 129
iron oxide 118

kerosene106
Kevlar 131
kilowatt-hours 178
kinetic energy 161

lactic acid 61
ladybirds 32
lead 118
lead chromate 112–113

lead oxide 118
lead sulfide 118
leaves 20–21
left atrium 70
left ventricle 70
lens cameras 188–189
light bulbs 168–171
light-years 204
limestone 100, 104
loft insulation 173
LPG (liquefied petroleum gas) 106
lungs 62–63, 86

magnesium 18, 19
magnifying glasses 189
malleable materials 128
manganese (IV) oxide 105
mantle (Earth) 200
marble 100
materials 124–145
    ceramics 126, 132–133
    colloids 138–139
    composites 127, 134–135
    metals 118–119, 126, 128–129
    polymers 126, 130–131
measles 78
medical drugs 87
meiosis 13
membranes 13, 22, 23
metals 118–119, 126, 128–129
methane 99, 107, 149
microorganisms 78–79, 80–81
    food poisoning 82
    immune system 84
microscopes 189
microwaves 190, 191
milk 138
Milky Way 204
minerals 18–19, 26, 100
mitosis 13
mixtures 99
MMR vaccine 85
molecules 140
morphine 10, 79
mumps 78

naphtha 107
natural gas 149
neutralisation 110
neutrons 98
nicotine 86
nitrates 18, 19, 26, 27
nitrogen 65, 198
non-renewable energy 151
nuclear power 152–153, 159
nuclei (atoms) 98
nuclei (cells) 13, 44
nylon 12, 130–131, 134

optical devices 188–189
ores 118